# Psalms for Graduates

# Psalms for Graduates

## Brent D. Earles

 **BAKER BOOK HOUSE**
Grand Rapids, Michigan 49506

Copyright 1984 by
Baker Book House Company

ISBN: 0-8010-3426-4

Fourth printing, January 1988

Scripture quotations are from the New International Version, copyright © 1978 by the
New York International Bible Society, used by permission of Zondervan Bible Pub-
lishers.

Illustrations by Dwight Baker

Printed in the United States of America

The author gratefully acknowledges permission to use the following copy-
righted material:

| page 11 | Excerpt from "Murphy's Law" poster. © Celestial Arts, Berkeley, Calif. |
| --- | --- |
| page 17 | Quotation from *Hide or Seek* by James Dobson. © 1974, 1979 by Fleming H. Revell Company. |
| pages 27-29 | Quotation from *For Mature Adults Only* by Norman C. Habel, pp. 28, 29. © 1969 by Fortress Press, Philadelphia, Pa. |
| page 42 | Quotation from *Falling Into Greatness* by Lloyd John Ogilvie, pp. 20-21. © 1984 by Thomas Nelson Publishers, Nashville, Tenn. |
| page 72 | Excerpt from lyrics, "Que Sera, Sera." © 1956 by Jay Livingston and Raymond Evans. |
| page 75 | Excerpt from *Knowing God's Will and Doing It* by J. Grant Howard, pp. 13-15. © 1976 by The Zondervan Corporation. |
| page 82 | Excerpt from lyrics, "Time in a Bottle," © 1974 by Blendingwell Music, Inc., Englewood, N.J., and MCA, Inc., New York. |
| page 87 | Quotation from *When I Relax, I Feel Guilty* by Tim Hansel. © 1979 by David C. Cook Publishing House, Elgin, Ill. |
| page 138 | Excerpt from lyrics, "Count Your Blessings Instead of Sheep," by Irving Berlin. © 1952, renewed 1980 by Irving Berlin. Reprinted by permission of Irving Berlin Music Corporation. |

# Contents

# Introduction

Athanasius, a giant of early Christian history, once wrote, "Most Scripture speaks to us, while the Psalms speak for us." Psalms is a book of comfort and courage. In it every type of emotion is outpoured, and every sort of concern is expressed. Reading its splendid poetry opens the gateway to the heart and unravels the challenges of life.

This is more of a topical search in the treasures of the Psalms. You will find there is a message in its order. Naturally, all people face the struggles and triumphs, puzzles and praises, we are about to consider. However, these have been carefully chosen to apply to your unique perspective on life. For a special group of people— *graduates!*

Like a nature walk, these chapters will take you on a trial run of life's adventures. You will get a crack at walking across the dry deserts of loneliness and brokenness, where you will experience a thirst felt only in the soul. Then, stepping into the throne room of prayer and the quiet chamber of worship, that deep thirst will be quenched. Your journey will take you to the mountain peaks of glory and conquest, then into the valleys of fear and urgency. Along cool streams of love, you will feel serenity as only God can give it, and the might of his power will comfort you as you rest under his shadow. Looking into the hidden creeks of destiny, you will see your own reflection and be challenged to live life as God designed it to be lived. With praise and thanksgiving you will feel like singing, because the richness of life will take shape for the first time.

Remember, though, this is only a trial run. It isn't the real McCoy. And while you are sure to discover these many life experiences, each person finds them differently. They are unique for each individual, just as each of you is one of a kind.

So come—adventure with me. Step into the dearest book of the human heart—*the Psalms!* Catch the drama. Your own life will not be so different. In fact, later on I expect you will come back to see your reflection in its quiet waters. Time and again you will return.

Now close your eyes and meditate. Meditation is merely calm thinking and is crucial to understanding Psalms. Meditate. Imagine you are looking at a weather-beaten house on some remote part of the planet. Most of it has caved in. Little paint remains on the splitting gray boards. What does is brittle and peeling. Beneath it is a twisted foundation. Bent over with the weight of time and heaviness, it appears about to crumble. Meditate harder. Envision it. When you open your eyes, read the next page, and you will be there. . . .

# 1 **Foundations**

## *Ground Floor*

*When the foundations are being destroyed, What can the righteous do? (Ps. 11:3).*

It used to be a lovely home, but now it is gradually falling apart. The old structure would probably be as good as ever, had it not been abandoned. Sure, time took its toll. Weather-beaten, too. It barely resembles the showplace it once was.

See it there in your mind's eye. Meditate on it until it comes into focus. Decayed and overrun with mice and rats and creepy bugs, the walls are awry atop the caved-in foundation. Jagged boards jut out in all directions. Weeds have grown high enough to nearly hide the house, as if to protect it from shame and embarrassment in the eyes of onlooking passersby. If it could speak, it would cry for help—if it could think, it would wonder why.

Depressing scenario, isn't it? We've all seen the remains of a house similar to this description. However, as I meditated on Psalm 11:3, I did not envision a house. In fact, in my description I did not have a building in mind at all.

What then? A society. *Our* society. By now it is obvious to you that our foundations are bursting apart. Take a closer look and you'll see what I mean:

Today many popular athletes are paid four to five times as much as our President.

Our school systems have become a thorn of concern because of poor quality.

Marriage has lost credibility, due largely to divorce and permissive lifestyles.

Sexuality is on constant reckless display wherever we turn.

Suicide is becoming the solution to more people's problems, especially the young (16–25) and the old (over 65).

Serious crimes and violence increase, and our jails and prisons bulge at the seams.

Wife abuse, child abuse, drug and alcohol abuse, are startlingly real every day.

Churches and Christian schools have squared off in more legal conflicts with state and federal government than any time in our history.

Economic factors such as spending, budgeting, interest rates, and inflation have become as difficult to control as a wet hen loose in the coop.

Cults and strange religions are on the rise.

Worldwide, there are winds of war and storms of terrorism, while we fight back fears of one all-out hurricane of destruction—nuclear holocaust.

That brings the picture into fine focus, doesn't it? The question is, when these foundations are being destoyed what can people who love the Lord do about it? That question is complicated by the fact that it's hard to keep good foundations in our own individual, personal lives. You know what I mean, don't you? It seems as if there is always something wanting to fall apart.

Murphy knows. He speaks for us all in his comical but true "laws of life." Here's a list of "Murphy's Laws." While you're laughing, see if you find a crack in your own mortar:

Nothing is as easy as it looks; everything takes longer than you think; if anything can go wrong it will.

A day without a crisis is a total loss.

The other line always moves faster.

The chance of the bread falling with the peanut-butter-and-jelly side down is directly proportional to the cost of the carpet.

Inside every large problem is a series of small problems struggling to get out.

Whatever hits the fan will not be evenly distributed.

No matter how long or hard you shop for an item, after you've bought it, it will be on sale somewhere cheaper.

Any tool dropped while repairing a car will roll underneath to the exact center.

Friends come and go, but enemies accumulate.

The light at the end of the tunnel is the headlamp of an oncoming train.

Day by day little things chip away at the foundations at home, at work, at school; morally, ethically, and spiritually. But we shouldn't be discouraged. There is a bedrock that is safe to build on.

Jesus closed his Sermon on the Mount with a lesson in civil engineering. He mentioned the principles of that bedrock:

> "Therefore everyone who hears these words of mine and puts them into practice is like a wise man who built his house on the rock. The rain came down, the streams rose, and the winds blew and beat against that house; yet it did not fall, because it had its foundation on the rock. But everyone who hears these words of mine and does not put them into practice is like a foolish man who built his house on sand. The rain came down, the streams rose, and the winds blew and beat against that house and it fell with a great crash."
>
> Matt. 7:24–27

Jesus wasn't talking about building houses. He meant the architecture of a life. Upon what foundation should a life be constructed? Latch on to these verses:

> For no one can lay any foundation other than the one already laid, which is Jesus Christ.
>
> 1 Cor. 3:11

> Nevertheless, God's solid foundation stands firm, sealed with this inscription: "The Lord knows those who are his," and, "Everyone who confesses the name of the Lord must turn away from wickedness."
>
> 2 Tim. 2:19

So, then, we have a positive answer to the psalmist's chilling question. What *can* the righteous do? They can build their lives and futures upon the One True Rock—Jesus Christ. And they can challenge those on sinking sand all about them to do the same.

As the torch is gradually passed to your generation, if you dare to be so determined, perhaps Isaiah's prophecy will apply to you:

> "Your people will rebuild the ancient ruins and will raise up the age-old foundations; you will be called Repairer of Broken Walls, Restorer of Streets with Dwellings."
>
> Isa. 58:12

Who knows? Maybe even Murphy can find some hope.

## 2 Sover[...]

### God "Reins"

*I will come and proclaim your mighty acts, O Sovereign*
*LORD; I will proclaim your righteousness, yours alone"*
*(Ps. 71:16).*

It was Shakespeare who made Marc Antony say these words at Caesar's funeral: "If you have tears, prepare to shed them now."

Every generation thinks it coined the phrase, "We didn't get the world into this mess, but now you expect us to get it out." Each new "establishment" has had its own share of turmoil to deal with.

Maybe you see yours as the worst ever. After all, while there have been threats of nuclear war before, never has the danger of widespread destruction seemed so imminent. The idea of hundreds of

13

ling thousands of miles over
rror movies rolled into one. If
ere to say, "Don't shed them

e all-powerful God. He is in
ould bring comfort and as-
en may make evil plans, but
rs, and no man can prevent
lerful to know that no matter
s, God is still in charge?
olding the *reins* of the uni-
sovereign, God can move in
e only pleases to do what is
ough thoughts are easy to
flipping coins in heaven to
universe in his hands.
crets about God? He never
oing on. God never worries
that things will not work out. He never gets confused. He never says,
"Wow! Things are really jammed up down there. I don't know what to
do next." In fact, he never frets over decisions at all. He knows what
he will do before the circumstances ever arise, because he knows
what the circumstances will be before they happen.

Want to know some neater stuff? God knows the exact count of
birds on earth. He knows which species live where and sees to it
they have plenty to eat. He knows precisely how many strands of
hair you have on your head, and he is interested in the minutest
detail of your life. In mine. In everyone's. To me that's exciting!

But how about tragedy and catastrophe? These both occur every
day. There are countless painful aspects of life:

Young children are kidnapped by the thousands each year; hundreds of them are abused in child pornography.

Senseless murders and brutalities occur routinely.

Innocent people die hourly in fires, car accidents, and other disasters.

Children, helpless and so full of happiness, are taken by incurable diseases.

All about us are crippled and handicapped people.

Where is God? If he is in control, why doesn't he do something? Doesn't he care? Is this his way of "getting even"? Has he turned his back and fallen deaf to all these hurts? If he permits these, who's to say he won't allow a nuclear demolition?

One of the greatest misunderstandings about God is his permissiveness. Since God allows certain things—his IQ is light-years above ours—naturally we want to blame him when things mess up. Here is where the misunderstanding comes in. God does not force his will upon people or upon our world. He doesn't hold a gun to anybody's head. Although he pleads through his Word for people to obey, he allows even evil men the freedom to make their own choices. In unexplainable tragedies God always has a purpose, which is usually beyond our brainpower to understand.

Therein lies the beauty of God's sovereignty. While the world appears to be flinging out of control toward collision with calamity, God has a calm grip on the reins. His design will be completed. His purposes will be fulfilled. He has never once lost control.

And we know that in all things God works for the good of those who love him, who have been called according to his purpose.

Rom. 8:28

Hard to grasp? Maybe this illustration will help. Imagine two chess players, one a magnificent master, the other a simple amateur. The master has memorized hundreds of first moves, war plays, traps, and closing moves. However, the rookie moves with wild abandon without much skill. Both are free to move as they please, and yet the master is coolly in absolute control. He is never upset or

15

intimidated by the recklessness of his opponent, but uses every silly, careless move to accomplish his own desires. All along, the rookie learns the lesson of his life.

God is like that master chess player. As people live selfishly and determine to do certain things with their lives, he allows it. Sometimes those moves bring tragedy and pain and regret. The Master then makes his move. Working through the broken pieces we have caused, he lovingly offers to rebuild us to a more beautiful condition. He wins, but we do not lose in the process. Ultimately, if we yield to him, we win with him!

> As it is written: "For your sake we face death all day long; we are considered as sheep to be slaughtered."
> No, in all these things we are more than conquerors through him who loved us.
>
> Rom. 8:36–37

Even when yours might seem like hopeless days, full of breathless situations, you have the assurance that God reigns. That is to say, he holds the reins. Be confident in him.

If you have any tears to shed, you can dry them now.

# 3 **Self-Value**

## *Mirror, Mirror*

*I praise you because I am fearfully and wonderfully made;*
*your works are wonderful, I know that full well (Ps. 139:14).*

*H*ide or Seek, by Dr. James Dobson, is bound to become a classic on the problem of inferiority. It is a tremendous inspiration to becoming the unique you that God designed. Dr. Dobson relates the story of a little boy named Chris, who had a facial deformity that had required plastic surgery. After being called "turtle" because of his lip, little Chris felt as if God hated him, even that he would probably end up in hell!

Touching a raw nerve, Dr. Dobson goes on to say:

Can't you feel Chris's loneliness and despair? How unfortunate for a seven-year-old child to believe that he is already hated by the

17

entire universe! What a waste of the potential that existed at the moment of his birth. What unnecessary pain he will bear throughout his lifetime. Yet Chris is merely one more victim of a stupid, inane system of evaluating human worth—a system which stresses attributes which cannot be obtained by the majority of our children. Instead of rewarding honesty, integrity, courage, craftsmanship, humor, motherhood, loyalty, patience, diligence, or other virtues which were praised in earlier times, we reserve maximum credit for bright young people who "look good" on a beach. Isn't it now appropriate that we abandon this needless discrimination?

In stark contrast to this youngster, I counseled at length just tonight with a seventy-five-year-old woman who feels worthless. She fears becoming bedridden in the nursing home where she lives. She anguishes over the possibility of losing the coordination to feed herself. Since life has lost its luster for her, she cannot help but question whether it is worth continuing.

Can you feel *her* pain? I think most of us can understand the hurt of little Chris and of the elderly woman, because their agony has at least once before been our own. The "inferiority epidemic" is all too familiar. No age escapes. Especially not graduates!

In his book *Is There Life After High School?*, Ralph Keyes points out that high-school memories stay with us for a lifetime. Past embarrassments plague us, and cherished moments play back positive messages. Why does high school stick with us? Probably because it brings the first point-blank showdown we have—facing ourselves. During this time we want so badly to belong, to be a hero. Failure of any kind burns into us like a brand. We rarely forget.

All along, you are building a mental image of yourself. Once the graduation ceremonies are over—the tassel is moved, the cap and gown put away, the "pomp and circumstance" send-off becomes a pretty memory—you have to wake up in the morning to look in the mirror.

Today, I want you to look closer. Not only into the bathroom mirror at your outside body, but deeper inside at the person who is really you. What do you think about yourself? Go ahead and be honest. This might become the initial step in shaping your future.

Sounds strange, I know. It is odd that the Psalms would focus this clearly on "self." Man usually has no difficulty in banging his own drum. That is exactly the problem. Selfishness begs only for a trip to the hit parade. It seeks a temporary thrill or worldly status, but never actually meets the need of the inner you. Yearning to get out of each of us is God's unique design in our lives. An exciting awareness of our true value is the key to releasing this treasure.

Once this inner vision lights up, the response is much like the psalmist's: "Wow! God made me to be special. Whether great or small, I have a wonderful role to fill in life. For this I was specifically made!" This is the heart of self-value. Not so much the "I'm okay, you're okay" mentality, but the "I am God's craftsmanship" celebration.

Popeye, the old cartoon character, might have said it better than we ever thought: "I yam what I yam, 'cause I yam what I yam!" That's simple self-acceptance. Being comfortable with the person God made is the biggest stride toward feelings of self-worth.

This "self" stuff can get out of hand, though. When it does, pride and conceit devalue us. Alan Reuter has written a sharp book on this subject, *Who Says I'm OK?* He tries to make some sense out of this self-concept business. Self-centeredness draws you away from the blueprint God wrote in you. Letting God be in charge eventually brings about the longest-lasting achievements. Those are the eternal ones!

Nothing else makes us so valuable. That God centers his attention on each of us individually is the most fantastic marvel of all. He cares about us. We are his fascination, the objects of his love—his magnificent obsession. This is what Martin Luther meant when he said, "God does not love us because we are valuable. We are valuable because God loves us."

Now it is time to take a look into that mirror. This might not be so easy, because we've all experienced an episode like Chris's nightmare of self-doubt and rejection. But it is these negative "mind cassettes" that echo in our brains, keeping our esteem low. God wants to replace those feelings of worthlessness with dignity. He wants to erase those tapes and record his symphony in our lives.

When that happens, the hiding stops—and the seeking begins!

"Didst thee ever talk to anyone who has seen them?"

"No."

"Then dost thee believe thee has any?" The wise Quaker's double meaning killed two birds with one stone—rationalizing and pride.

God made it hard for people to deny him. He painted his existence all ⟨over⟩ our universe.

> ⟨...⟩ known about God is plain to them, because God
> ⟨...⟩ hem. For since the creation of the world God's
> ⟨...⟩ ternal power and divine nature—have been
> ⟨...⟩ tood from what has been made, so that

Rom. 1:19–20

⟨...⟩ sun is a mere smidgen of his
⟨...⟩ he doesn't sleep at night.
⟨...⟩ of his wisdom, while the
⟨...⟩ the puniest details
⟨...⟩ power, the hav⟨...⟩
⟨...⟩ bit of G⟨...⟩

so⟨...⟩
sign⟨...⟩
is a Go⟨...⟩

The e⟨...⟩
tence, beca⟨...⟩
him are data a⟨...⟩
faith. His "scien⟨...⟩
overlook the obvi⟨...⟩

This really hits h⟨...⟩
scientist who figured ou⟨...⟩
so simple that it sounds si⟨...⟩

# 4 Atheism
## The Fool's Creed

*The fool says in his heart, "There is no God" (Ps. 14:1).*

It has been said that an atheist can't find God for the same reason that a thief can't find a policeman. That pretty well sums up atheism. As supersmart as many atheists have strutted around, God strips their proud minds to shame with one tiny word—*fool!* And isn't it an appropriate word? For whatever so-called brilliant theories people can whip up about our origin, nothing seems quite so stupid as to say, "There is no God." Not that the Lord is a name-caller. He isn't. By using this word, God was not reducing himself to childishness, arguing back, "Here's mud in your eye for denying me. I'm going to call you a fool. Now, how does that feel?" No, no! That's not the idea at all.

hand-made a scale model of our solar system. The sun was in the center, and the various planets were set in their orbital tracks.

One day an old friend stopped by to visit Newton. Upon entering his study, the fellow scientist spied Sir Isaac's masterpiece and got excited, "My! That is a tremendous replica! Who made it?"

"Nobody," said Newton, going about his business matter-of-factly, as he remembered that his colleague was an atheist.

"Come now," the visitor smiled, "you must think that I'm a fool. Of course somebody made this solar system. And I must say he's quite a genius," meaning to praise Sir Isaac.

Isaac turned to face his friend and spoke very directly: "This thing is a tiny imitation of our grand system whose laws you and I know, and I am not able to convince you that this mere toy has no designer or creator; but you profess to believe that the original from which this copy was made came into existence without a Creator. Now tell me, by what sort of logic do you reach such inconsistent conclusions?"

> God hast a presence, and that ye may see
> In the fold of the flower, the leaf of the tree;
> In the sun of the noon-day, the star of the night;
> In the storm-cloud of darkness, the rainbow of light;
> In the waves of the ocean, the furrows of land;
> In the mountains of granite, the atom of sand;
> Turn where ye may, from the sky to the sod,
> Where can ye gaze that ye see not a God?
>
> —*C. H. Spurgeon*

A policeman is the last person a thief wants to see, because of his crime, the fear of capture, and what justice will mean. That is exactly why atheists don't want to believe in God. They, like all of us, are sinners before a perfect God. They also figured out long ago that God is not fond of sin. So, it's either live a life of sin, which brings a guilty conscience, or seek God's forgiveness. Opting for the self-life, the atheist denies God to avoid feeling guilty.

noon he
not believe
creatures of
the obviously
"Didst thee eve
edly.
"No, but others hav
wisely accept what they
"Oh, thou wilt believe o
"Absolutely! It has to be s
The old man raised his eyeb
brim of his black Quaker hat, then
see thy brains?"
"Well," the doubter chuckled, "no.'

The sad truth is that denying fire is hot doesn't prevent a person from getting burned. "On earth are atheists many/In hell there is not any."

# 5 Faith

## *Mountain Moving*

*Some trust in chariots and some in horses, but we trust in the name of the LORD our God (Ps. 20:7).*

In *Three Steps Forward, Two Steps Back,* Charles Swindoll makes a statement that can transform the "I give up" attitude into superb faith. He says, "We are all faced with a series of great opportunities brilliantly disguised as impossible situations."

Opportunities? But how we dread tough circumstances. They are painful, maddening, and sometimes downright disgusting. Most people with a sound mind wouldn't keep on trying to succeed in the face of such distress. Opportunities should be exciting, pleasant, and vibrant. So we think. Too often we throw up our hands and scream when we should be zeroing in on the target through the eyes of faith. Doubtfulness kills opportunity, making the situation appear that much more "impossible."

Frankly, I'm shook up by the trends I see these days. Are we getting soft? Afraid to be daring? Do we believe that great tasks are finished easily? Have we forgotten that our God is the God of the impossible? Has self-satisfaction gotten a grip on us, strangling out the dreams of brighter tomorrows? Smothering our faith that God wants to accomplish wonderful things in our lives for his name's sake?

Maybe failure has checkered our faith. And it's hard to keep believing when failure after failure floods in. Norman Habel's *For Mature Adults Only* records the prose penned by a young man who felt beaten, drained of faith in himself and in God to help him. Here are his tearful words:

> No one pays any attention to me
> or what I say, Lord.
>> I'm nobody, I guess.
> I haven't done anything important
> or made anything
> or won anything.
> No one listens when I talk,
> No one asks my opinion.
>> I'm just there
>> like a window
>> or a chair.
>
> I tried to build a boat once,
> but it fell apart.
> I tried to make the baseball team,
> but I always threw past third base.
> I wrote some articles
> for our school paper,
> but they didn't want them.
> I even tried out for the school play,
> but the other kids laughed

when I read my lines.
    I seem to fail
    at everything.

I don't try anymore
because I'm afraid to fail.
And no one likes to fail
all the time.

If only there was something I could do,
something I could shout about,
something I could make
that was my work,
only mine.
And people would say,
"David did that!"
And my parents would say,
"We're proud of you, son!"

But I can't do anything.
Everyone else is so much better
at everything
than I am.
The more I fail
the more it eats away at me
    until I feel weak inside.
    I feel like I'm nothing.
Lord, the world seems full of heroes
and idols and important people.

Where are all the failures?
Where are they hiding?
Where are people like me?
Do you ever fail, Lord?
Did you?
Do you know how I feel?

Do you know what it's like

when everyone looks up at you and says:
"He's a failure."

When defeat talks, that's what it sounds like. Do you know why such agonizing frustration creeps in? It's more than a loss of faith. It's because all along too much attention was centered on what "I" can do instead of on what God can do.

I'm not picking on this fellow who poured out his heart to God. We've all been struck before by a similar kind of lightning. In fact, he asks a very important question: "Do you ever fail, Lord?"

What do you think? Does God ever goof up? Does he ever say: "Oops! I really blew it this time." Does God throw in the towel? Never.

Is anything too hard for the LORD? . . .

Gen. 18:14

"Ah, Sovereign LORD, you have made the heavens and the earth by your great power and outstretched arm. Nothing is too hard for you."

Jer. 32:17

We need to believe that. That's what faith is all about—knowing that God is able to do things that we could never do in a million years. And believing that he is willing and wants to do them on our behalf, if we trust him and yield to him.

Jesus was approached one day by a man whose situation seemed impossible. His son was possessed by a demon. The boy often jerked about in violent convulsions. Foam came out of his mouth. It was an ugly sight. Let's pick up with the story just as it reads:

Jesus asked the boy's father, "How long has he been like this?"
"From childhood," he answered. "It has often thrown him into fire or water to kill him. But if you can do anything, take pity on us and help us."
"If you can?" said Jesus. "Everything is possible for him who believes."

29

Immediately the boy's father exclaimed, "I do believe; help me overcome my unbelief!"

Mark 9:21–24

Overcoming unbelief is the first step to moving mountains in your life. Because nothing is impossible with God when you believe. Here's the wonder of it all. *It doesn't take much faith to experience God's power in your life.* Jesus said, ". . . I tell you the truth, if you have faith as small as a mustard seed, you can say to this mountain, 'Move from here to there' and it will move. Nothing will be impossible for you" (Matt. 17:20–21).

Got any mountains to move? *Trust in the name of the Lord our God.* He turns the impossible into the incredible!

# 6 Thirstiness

## Water, Water, Everywhere

*As the deer pants for streams of water, so my soul pants for you, O God. My soul thirsts for God, for the living God. When can I go and meet with God? (Ps. 42:1–2).*

From Samuel Taylor Coleridge's long-spun *The Rime of the Ancient Mariner* come these famous words:

> Water, water, everywhere,
> And all the boards did shrink.
> Water, water, everywhere
> Nor any drop to drink.

We are thirsty people in an ocean of contamination. God places within everyone a yearning for fulfillment, a groaning for satisfaction, a hunger for completion. Our complicated world flashes with hundreds of cures. None of them works. And yet their popularity never ends.

People actually drink contamination to quench that thirst! How they sink! There's the money trough where some burn themselves out making as much as they can. In spite of all it can buy, there are some riches that money will never afford—love, joy, and peace.

Fame is the drink that others seek. To have a name, a position, recognition, applause, even envy from the less accomplished. This is the dirty water a parched soul might reach for.

When life's battles get toughest, some will turn to escape the rapids—alcohol, drugs, illicit sex. But this white-water ride is filled with one dangerous waterfall after another. The rider goes down, down, down. Then under.

Any cup the world has to offer eventually becomes empty. Isaiah's words describe those who try to find relief from the world's waters: "As when a hungry man dreams that he is eating, but he awakens, and his hunger remains; as when a thirsty man dreams that he is drinking, but he awakens faint, with his thirst unquenched" (Isaiah 29:8).

Then why did God give us this craving for contentment? Because only *he* can satisfy it. Meaning that when we finally get thirsty for a relationship with him, he will give us a long, cold drink from the springs of living water.

A scene from the life of Jesus pinpoints this perfectly. He was traveling through Samaria and stopped in a town called Sychar. A famous Jew named Jacob, from the Old Testament, had built a well there hundreds of years ago. Jesus sat down by that well. Let's pick up with the story:

> When a Samaritan woman came to draw water, Jesus said to her, "Will you give me a drink?" (His disciples had gone into the town to buy food.)

The Samaritan woman said to him, "You are a Jew and I am a Samaritan woman. How can you ask me for a drink?" (For Jews do not associate with Samaritans.)

Jesus answered her, "If you knew the gift of God and who it is that asks you for a drink, you would have asked him and he would have given you living water. . . . Everyone who drinks this water will be thirsty again, but whoever drinks the water I give him will never thirst. Indeed, the water I give him will become in him a spring of water welling up to eternal life."

John 4:7–10, 13

That water quenches thirst. It is what Jesus meant when he said, "Blessed are those who hunger and thirst for righteousness, for they will be filled" (Matt. 5:6). And later, when he said, "I am the bread of life. He who comes to me will never go hungry, and he who believes in me will never be thirsty" (John 6:35).

The journey of life is a desert without Christ. It runs us dry. Mirages disappear before our eyes, and we stand weary in the dust of our humanity. It is hard to hope. To dream. To find meaning and purpose. To know what to do next.

*Longing* is what we need today. Longing for God. Not for religious programs, nor churchmanship, nor bland sameness. Our age is dry, cracked ground yearning for a downpour. Instead of little spiritual games, there must be a quest for God himself.

That's missing, I'm afraid, in a lot of lives. Too many are hooked on "churchianity." Routine is easier. Plenty has already been tasted. Sadly, people who know Christ, and were once eager to know him better still, have lost that ache for closeness with Christ that had never yet been felt. A little became enough.

In *The Pursuit of God,* A. W. Tozer writes about this:

The stiff and wooden quality about our religious lives is a result of our lack of holy desire. Complacency is a deadly foe of all spiritual growth. Acute desire must be present or there will be no manifestation of Christ to His people. He waits to be wanted. Too bad that with many of us He waits so long, so very long, in vain.

Someone once said, "Christianity is either an acute fever or a dull habit." The psalmist had an acute fever. He was panicked by the distance between himself and God. God was too far away! He had to get closer!

I was in a large department store recently, looking at summer clothes. I noticed a little girl walking around all alone. Scanning for her parents, I saw no one nearby to whom she might belong. I watched her carefully. The world of clothes racks and counters was huge to her, and no doubt the store seemed like an unending expanse compared to her tiny world. She grew nervous. Then frightened. Then frantic! She began to cry softly. No one came. I directed a saleslady to her plight, thinking that a man might spook her even more than she already was. Soon she found rescue and was reunited with worried parents.

That's how the psalmist felt. Alone. Helpless. Tired. Afraid. Out of these powerful emotional pangs he reached for the Lord. Anything in him that was before a dull habit caught fire in a burning pursuit of God.

Are you thirsty? Does the vastness of the future blow-dry your throat? Has the flavor of the world's "cola" done little to absorb the pant of your breath? When you conclude your day, do you feel as if you are running in place, spinning your wheels?

Trading cups might be for you. The sparkle of God's water puts a sparkle into life. Follow hard after him. Run in his footsteps. Call out loud for him.

> Not for peace, not for power,
> Not for joy, and not for light;
> Not for truth, and not for knowledge,
> Not for courage for the fight,
> Not for strength to do Thy service,

Not for these my prayer shall be,
Not for any gifts or graces
But for Thee, Lord, just for Thee.
Make me lonely for Thy presence
Every earthly friend above;
Make me thirst for Thy indwelling,
Make me hungry for Thy love
'Til in full and free surrender
I shall yield my life to Thee
Only then in full perfection
Canst Thou give Thyself to me.
—*Annie Johnson Flint*

Water, water, everywhere, but Christ is the very best drink.

# 7 Worship

## Land of Ahhhs!

*Ascribe to the LORD the glory due his name; worship the
LORD in the splendor of his holiness (Ps. 29:2).*

The throne of God sits in the true land of ahhhs!—heaven.
With a galaxy of glory adorning that place, the entire atmosphere is
one of majesty. In it are the tree of life and the river of life; the crystal
sea and streets of gold; the jasper and ruby, diamond and sapphire.
An emerald rainbow encircles the throne. Six-winged angels cry,
"Holy! Holy! Holy! Lord God Almighty!" With two wings they shield
their faces from a radiance too glorious to behold; with two wings
they cover their beings; with two wings they fly. Remarkable. Hard to
imagine. Difficult to grasp.

But this is not the only place where worship of God happens.

Every speck of creation seen by man has its own unique and breathtaking ahhhs! that can inspire worship. When a massive lake lies placid, reflecting a bright blue sky filled with cream-puff clouds—that's inspirational. When mountains stand proud above fog-covered valleys below—that's show stopping. When a shooting star races across the night skyway in a momentary streak of light—that's eye-catching. These and many more treasures of nature invite us to the chambers of worship.

No, worship is not just a Sunday affair. Or only a church experience. It should be the natural heartbeat of life itself, although Sunday and church should certainly be spiced up with authentic heaven-on-earth worship. It is terrible when church services plod along like an overweight, overloaded mule. Everything about the services should be geared toward getting in touch with God, so that the tired and tempted can leave refueled and ready to live.

God wants our worship. He wants no other—whether it be person or object, statue or possession—to have the attention due his name. That would be idolatry. We think of idolatry as being some weird ritual done in an obscure jungle where no "civilized" person has even been. But it's everywhere. Because anytime God gets replaced, guess what? That's idolatry.

Just what replaces God? Well, nothing should. But at various times, with different people, nearly everything does. Think with me. Can you see how these things sometimes dethrone God in our society?

Career—the plight of the workaholic

Sports—the altar of recreation

Possessions—the carved image of materialism

Heroes—the magnet of charisma

Busyness—the power of "plans"

Money—the glitter of gold

Self—the trumpet of humanity

None of these is wrong, if kept in check. It is when they break loose that the ahhhs! become ughhhs!

The question is: How do we worship God? What is worship? First, and probably foremost, is the need for love. In *That Incredible Christian,* A. W. Tozer says, "It is quite impossible to worship God without loving Him. This love is the heart of the art of genuine worship. Deep down within you do you love God?" Maybe you remember the commandment Jesus cited as being the greatest: "Love the Lord your God with all your heart and with all your soul and with all your mind" (Matt. 22:37).

A story is told about a man who dreamed he was escorted to church by an angel. When they arrived, the place was packed, but a strange mystery occurred. The organist appeared to be playing happily, but no music came out. As the choir and congregation sang, their lips moved, but no sounds were audible. The preacher delivered his sermon, but once again the room was as silent as if no one were there at all.

The man was dumbfounded. He tugged at the angel and asked, "What is wrong here? Why are we able to see what is happening, but unable to hear what they're saying?" You can imagine his astonishment.

The angel's answer in the dream was very pointed. He said, "You can't hear anything, because there is nothing to be heard. It's empty. The words are offered from empty hearts. This is the way God sees the service. He does not hear what comes from the lips only, but what comes from the heart of love."

Suddenly, the man could hear a tiny voice in the back pew. He could barely make out the prayer. It was a little girl, and she was praying, "My Father, which art in heaven, you have a pretty name. . . ."

The angel spoke up, "The reason why you can hear her is that her words come genuinely from the love she has for God. You are hearing what God is hearing."

Thought provoking, huh? How much of today's worship would fall into that silent charade? How much would spring forth from simple love like that little girl showed?

Another aspect of worship is admiration. This is a step above loving God for what he has done to bless us. This is loving God for *who* he is. Too many never reach this level of worship.

One evening Moses was sitting in the desert minding his own business. All of a sudden a bramble bush caught fire, but the bush did not burn up. It kept getting brighter, until Moses heard God speak. God said, "Take off your shoes, because you are on holy ground."

What made that place holy so fast? I mean, ten seconds ago it was plain sand. Now it's holy. Why? Because God was there. His presence made it an altar of worship. Not because of anything he had done, but because of who he is.

Moses, at that burning bush, later asked God to give himself a name that could be told to the Israelites and to the Egyptian Pharaoh who was holding God's people captive. God said, "I am who I am." In other words, we might say that God is God because everything about him is perfect and always has been. Always will be. That makes me sigh "Ahhh!" in amazement.

Let me share some of the attributes of God that invite admiration and adoration:

*Holiness*. God is absolutely free from sin, immeasurably pure.

*Omnipotence*. God has infinite power. Figuring his capabilities would melt down a computer.

*Immutability*. This is an uncommon word. It means that God never changes. He remains totally, constantly God.

*Omnipresence*. God knows to the smallest detail everything about everything and everyone, everywhere, at all times, because he is present everywhere at once. Wow! Did you catch all of that?

*Justice*. God is absolutely fair, even when we think he is not.

39

*Mercy*. God is tender and compassionate.

Just to name a few. God is great! He does not have to do anything to be worthy of our worship. Being himself is quite enough.

The secret of enjoying worship is regularity. The psalmist mentions several times that he met with God daily, even three times a day—morning, noon, and night. Not a bad schedule for worship, as long as it shines with realness—authenticity. If it's fake, it's inaudible.

More often the psalmist notes that he met with God to start his day. That will breathe new oxygen into you spiritually. Plunging into heaven for breakfast is bound to put snap, crackle, and pop back into life!

> Still, still with Thee, when purple morning breaketh,
>     When the bird waketh, and the shadows flee;
> Fairer than the morning, lovelier than daylight,
>     Dawns the sweet consciousness, I am with Thee.
>
> Alone with Thee, amid the mystic shadows,
>     The solemn hush of nature newly born;
> Alone with Thee in breathless adoration;
>     In the calm dew and freshness of the morn.
>
> As in the dawning o'er the waveless ocean,
>     The image of the morning-star doth rest,
> So in this stillness, Thou beholdest only
>     Thine image in the waters of my breast.
>
> When sinks the soul, subdued by toil, to slumber,
>     Its closing eyes look up to Thee in prayer;
> Sweet the repose, beneath Thy wings o'er shadowing,
>     But sweeter still to wake and find Thee there.
>                                         —*Harriet Beecher Stowe*

In the land of ahhhs! the bush is always burning.

# ⑧ Selah

## Shhh!

*I remembered you, O God, and I groaned; I mused, and my spirit grew faint. Selah (Ps. 77:3).*

Notice the word at the end of the verse. It shows up seventy-one times in the Book of Psalms. It is a poetic word. It is a musical word. It is a word we need to mix into our lifestyle. *Selah.*

What does it mean? Actually, most Bible scholars are not sure. Since it shows up only in Psalms, which were originally songs that Old Testament believers sang, it is widely accepted that *selah* was some sort of musical notation. Quite likely it marked a rest. For our understanding, as we read the Psalms, *selah* says, "Stop! Be silent and concentrate on what you just read. Let it soak in. Mull it over. Meditate."

There's that word again—meditate. *Selah* and meditation are not

41

so very different. "Meditate" was used in the Hebrew language in fascinating ways. Lloyd John Ogilvie uncovers some of those usages in his book, *Falling into Greatness:*

> The same word is used in Scripture for the young lion growling over its prey, for the murmuring of a dove, and as a synonym for "to remember and muse on." It is frequently used for a cow chewing its cud, a creature who masticates its food thoroughly. What is implied by the psalmist is that our meditation is to make the law our nature and character. We are to be immersed, soaked thoroughly, inundated with the truth of God's Word.

Meditation is not "mystical." It is not yoga. It does not involve sitting on the floor Indian-style, with wrists resting against your knees as forefinger and thumb form a circle. It is not a trance.

*Selah* is merely a stop sign. It warns us not to breeze past the words we just read. We are prone to daydream as we read. The sentences go through our eyes. Our eyes go down the page, but we don't remember what we read. Ever done that? If you're doing it now, then back up and reread.

A popular commercial about the importance of education tells us, "A mind is a great thing to waste." God's Word teaches something similar to that. Put *selah* to work on these verses:

> But I am afraid that just as Eve was deceived by the serpent's cunning, your *minds* may somehow be led astray from your sincere and pure devotion to Christ.
>
> 2 Cor. 11:3, *italics mine*

> Do not conform any longer to the pattern of this world, but be transformed by the renewing of your *mind*.
>
> Rom. 12:2, *italics mine*

> Set your *minds* on things above, not on earthly things.
>
> Col. 3:2, *italics mine*

> Therefore, prepare your *minds* for action. . . .
>
> 1 Peter 1:13, *italics mine*

I think it is safe to say that God wants us to take good care of our minds. They should not be wasted on worldliness or on wild living. To grow, a mind must be fed some chewy food.

How do you do that? By *selah*. By stopping, coming aside, and saturating your thoughts with God's Word. By meditating on verses that you enjoy and also on those you have difficulty understanding. It isn't kid stuff, is it? This is a new level of maturity. Willing to take the challenge?

Just thinking about Bible verses may not seem too appealing. I don't blame you. But there are ways to help meditation that can be fun. Let me throw out a few ideas, and then you can design your own game plan for renewing your mind:

*Memorizing.* That probably sounds boring and like too much effort. It's not that bad. By jotting down a verse on a little pocket card, you could memorize as many verses a week as you'd like. Whenever convenient, you can pull the verse out, mull it over, and stick it back into your pocket. This gets the Word right into the thick of life itself, giving it an opportunity to meet the struggles you face head-on. On top of that, once a verse is memorized, it's there to think about at the snap of your fingers.

*Visualizing.* Sometimes I like to close my eyes and construct a whole scene in my mind about what I just read. Take the story of David and Goliath, for example. I imagine an ugly giant who plays basketball for the Philistines. He's dressed in soot-black armor. He's got warts. He has a real stupid laugh. He's cocky and figures he's got the fight in the bag—especially when this teenage runt comes running up the hill in gym shorts, swinging a slingshot. Goliath laughs so hard he almost falls down. It's really hilarious until David starts screaming at him how God is going to make Goliath very dead. David rockets a rock between his eyes like a laser blast. The first great teenage champion! Visualizing makes the Bible exciting. It lets you be creative and imaginative.

*Personalizing.* Verses that are hard to visualize can sometimes become very helpful if made personal. By removing other names or pronouns and inserting your own name instead, the verse can become much more meaningful. Take this verse for example: "God is our refuge and strength, an ever present help in trouble" (Ps. 46:1).

It will sink in more, and mean more if you personalize it: "God is [John Smith's] refuge and strength, an ever present help in trouble." Put your own name in place of John Smith's. Claim the verse and it's yours. It does a lot more for the mind than personalized license plates do for cars.

Now those are just suggestions. Perhaps you have some ideas of your own. Fantastic! Just say, "Shhh!" to the world. Because the mind is a great thing to waste.

*Selah.*

# 9 Truth

## Signed, Sealed, Delivered

> *. . . guide me in your truth and teach me, for you are God my Savior, and all my hope is in you all day long* (Ps. 25:5).

An important question was once asked by a man who never really cared to know the answer. Not only was he too blind to see it, but he wasn't even looking. The man's name was Pilate. The person he asked was Jesus. The question was: "What is truth?" He was looking right at his answer.

Truth is hard for us to grasp. Not because it's complicated; it isn't. But mostly because truth must be lived to be learned. It must remain constant. Uncompromised. When blended with error, truth ceases to be truth, and a slippery substitute swallows it up—deception.

Situation ethics. That's today's biggest deception. It says that in

45

certain situations certain things are wrong. In other circumstances exactly the same things are all right. Situation ethics teaches that truth depends upon the situation.

How untrue. Truth is always right. Hard situations may inspire alternatives but should never alter truth. It is still never right to do a wrong in order to help the cause of right. We must not deceive ourselves. We cannot allow truth to be watered down. We cannot allow it to be changed into a lie.

And yet you may be wondering, "What is truth? Where can I find it. How can I experience it? Is there an example of how it works and affects lives?"

There are three lamps of truth, but all light one path. Each brightens the way for well-ordered steps. They don't compete with one another. One is not more truthful than another. In your quest to live life as it is meant to be, truth must shine for you. Don't get lost in the dark.

Look for light here:

**God's Word—Instructional Truth.** The psalmist wrote, "Your word is a lamp to my feet and a light for my path" (Ps. 119:105). Is this truth? Some say it is myth. Others say it makes good bedtime reading for children. That the heartwarming history stories from God are fairy tales. Would you believe it if I told you there are some who say it's only partly true? But Jesus never said that. He prayed to the Father, "Sanctify them by the truth; your word is truth" (John 17:17).

> What glory gilds the sacred page!
>  Majestic, like the sun;
> It gives a light to every age
>  It gives, but borrows none.
>
> The power that gave it still supplies
>  The gracious light and heat.
> Its truth upon the nations rise;
>  They rise but never set.
>
> Lord, everlasting thanks be Thine

In such a bright display
As makes a world of darkness shine
With beams of heavenly day.

Our souls rejoicingly pursue
The steps of him we love,
Till glory breaks upon our view
In brighter worlds above.
—*William Cowper*

Is there any doubt about the precious touch of God's Word? Is there any question about how it can fix broken lives? Is anyone able to argue sensibly that God's Word does not comfort and encourage, strengthen and rebuild?

It sets ablaze a light in our hearts and makes us a candle for the Lord.

***God's Son—Incarnate Truth.*** Jesus is a lamp of truth to give us light. He said, "I am the light of the world. Whoever follows me will never walk in darkness, but will have the light of life" (John 8:12). Truth in a body—Jesus. He is the perfect example of how truth can affect the lives of those it touches. In the short span of three years, the truth in sandals rocked Israel; which started a major quaking in the souls of men still being felt today. Jesus shook up humanity. He awed them. He awes us today. Because he is truth in living, breathing flesh. Is he really truth? Yes. He said, "I am the way and *the truth* and the life . . ." (John 14:6).

Christ, whose glory fills the skies
Christ, the true, the only Light,
Sun of righteousness, arise,
Triumph o'er the shade of night;
Dayspring from on high be near,
Daystar in my heart appear.
—*Charles Wesley*

Can I share a sad and unbelievable truth with you? "The light

47

shines in the darkness, but the darkness has not understood it" (John 1:5). That means that people cannot see truth when it jumps out to bite them. Pilate could not see.

*God's Spirit—Indwelling Truth.* The Holy Spirit lives within every Christian. Why? To guide us, like a light, into truth. Jesus taught this. "When he, the Spirit of truth, comes, he will guide you into all truth . . ." (John 16:13). He turns on the lights of understanding. Whenever our vision gets blurred, his lamp gets brighter. Shining the way, he gives us inner confidence. He confirms God's Word to us and spotlights the Lord's example. "And it is the Spirit who testifies, because the Spirit is the truth" (1 John 5:6). He helps us live the truth by giving us his power. But when we allow sin to dominate our lives, a shroud of darkness falls over us. He hides. He grieves. He is stifled. Our journey into truth is ruined with pitch-blackness. We must never lampshade his light, for then we fall into a deep ditch.

These three lamps are not Aladdin-type lamps. You cannot rub them for good luck or special wishes. Bargains are out. Do you know that some people actually try to make secret deals with God? They promise to follow truth in exchange for selfish blessings.

Truth is non-negotiable. I am often asked what the Bible has to say about this or that. I'll share a few verses to answer the question. Want to hear a shocker? Some people deny the verses I share. Or excuse them away. Or flat out reject them. Listen, this is serious stuff. God's truth is not up for a vote—"All those in favor of this being true, vote yes; all not in favor, vote no." That's nuts!

How vital to life is truth? Well, without it we're pretenders. We play-act. Phoney baloney overtakes realness. We become synthetic and plastic. We have to fasten life together with clothespins, because we get hung out to dry. We have to live at the speed of light to avoid seeing our emptiness in the mirror.

When Pilate finished his question, he walked away from Jesus. He signed the death papers. He sealed the crucifixion. He delivered

Jesus to the jeering crowd. There Jesus stood—Truth—signed, sealed, and delivered. But they could not grasp God's message.

A few hours later, as his life ebbed out on the cross, the Light of the World dimmed the light source of earth. It grew dark at midday. People trembled as jagged spears of lightning crashed to the ground in pitch-dark daytime. This symbolized the absence of truth.

Pilate had washed his hands, but his heart was as dirty as ever. Because he rejected the answer to his question.

# 10 Love

## Princess of Emotions

*I love the LORD, for he heard my voice; he heard my cry for mercy (Ps. 116:1).*

A woman visited the office of a magazine editor, bringing along several poems she had written. Her hopes were high that some of them could be sold for publication.

The editor didn't appear too excited at first: "Well, what are your poems about?"

"They're love poems." The woman had a glaze of romanticism over her eyes and in her tone of voice.

"That's just what the world needs," the editor said, as he leaned back in his chair, "another bunch of love poems." The sarcasm was evident. "Why don't you read me one?"

Her poem rambled with mushiness and starlit nights, candlelight and dreamy-eyed looks. The slushy rhyme was a bit more than the editor could handle.

"Just a minute," he stopped her rather abruptly, "this isn't what real love is all about! This moonlight-and-roses bit is for the silver screen. Love is taking on second jobs to help the family make ends meet. Love is enjoying simple times together, even when more romantic scenery is unavailable. Love is not just a fleeting feeling or only a tender moment. Love is able to endure the worst tempest. Go home and write a poem about old-fashioned love that sacrifices and scrapes and battles for survival against all odds—and wins!"

His little speech strikes a note about current trends in "love." How that word gets abused.

"I just *love* this steak."

"I *love* that dress."

"I *love* baseball."

"I *love* you."

Isn't it a bit bonkers to use the same word that expresses the princess emotion of the human heart to describe how we feel about both a person and a chunk of meat? When words get abused like this, they lose their clout. They become weak and meaningless.

What we need is a dust brush. To sweep away the grime that has cluttered today's understanding of love. A little spot remover wouldn't hurt either, for all the blemishes love has gotten from being thrown around. When the cleaning job is done, what sparkles in our gaze will be surprising. . . .

***One does not have to be loved to love.*** Jesus proved this. In spite of rejection and ridicule, Jesus loved so much that he gave his life to buy freedom for any and all who come to him. Jesus did not require that kindness be shown to him before he returned it. The warmth he had in his heart prompted him to reach out, even when his heart was breaking in two.

> To kiss the hands that smite,
> To pray for them that persecute,

To hear the voice of blame,
Reap undeserved shame,
  And still be mute—
  Is this not love?

To give for evil good,
  To learn what sacrifice can teach,
To be the scoffer's sport,
Nor strive to make retort,
  To angry speech—
  Is this not love?

To face the harsh world's harms,
  To brave its bitterness for years,
To be an unthanked slave,
And gain at last a grave
  Unwet by tears—
  Is this not love?

—*Susie Betts*

How very different from our I'll-love-you-if-you-love-me-back "me-ism" world. How dusty old-fashioned love has become!

**The lovely are not always the most lovable.** It's nice to be pretty. It's all right to be handsome. Style and grace, charm and intelligence, are good ingredients to have. But what causes people to zero in on the facial alignment of eyes, noses, teeth, and hair and forget all about the heart? When did the amount of love to be shown become dependent upon the way a body is pieced together?

Millions of people will never graduate from Aunt Sookie's Social Etiquette class. They may even seem sort of unlovable. Some of them forget to shave. Some are plain-looking or perhaps a little ugly. Some of them are not very bright. Others match dots with plaids when they get dressed. Some of them are poor. Some crippled. Some retarded. Some orphaned. Some full of hate.

These people respond to love, too. It just may take a little longer.

They have feelings down under their steel shields of protection. They cry. They hurt, although a thousand heartbreaks have taught them to avoid hoping for affection. If ever loved with reassuring love, they would be unable to run dry of the stored-up love they are prepared to return. The unlovable need to be loved.

***Expressing love is a wonderful way of making it stronger.*** It has been said that we wait until too late to tell people how much they mean to us. Too many have stood beside an open coffin, viewing the cold, lifeless body of a loved one with deep regret that certain words were not said sooner, when there was still time to warm an untold heart with love. Now it was too late.

There are dozens of ways to say it. Break free and say it today!

"You mean the world to me."

"Without you, life wouldn't be so full."

"Thank you for being you."

"You're a blessing from God."

"Your friendship is one of my best treasures."

"I'm glad I have someone like you to turn to."

"You're one of my favorite people."

"You make dull days bright."

Maybe you're old-fashioned enough to say it the old-fashioned way: *"I love you."*

***God loves us.*** And he wants us to love him. God does not force his love upon anyone. God does not barge into anyone's life. He does not manipulate or yank on people. He draws us to himself through his love. "This is love: not that we loved God, but that he loved us and sent his Son as an atoning sacrifice for our sins" (1 John 4:10).

This is the kind of love the world needs. All ages. All races. All creeds. All classes. Not a moonlight masquerade, but a heaven-sent serenade of the heart.

No one is able to express love quite like little children. So eager to

53

please. So innocent in saying grown-up words. Something my three-year-old daughter, Sara, said to me recently sums it up best. With toddler arms held wide open, in all seriousness she tilted her head to one side and tenderly said, "Daddy, I wuv you too much!"

O, that we had too much love.

# 11  Overshadowed

## *Spiritual Shade*

*He who dwells in the shelter of the Most High will rest in the shadow of the Almighty (Ps. 91:1).*

Want to hear a hilarious story? John Haggai tells about it in his book *How to Win Over Worry*. In Darlington, Maryland, Edith, a mother of eight, came home from a short visit at a neighbor's house. When she walked in the door, she saw her five youngest kids in a huddle. They were quietly admiring something together. She tried to slip closer to see what it was without interrupting them. She couldn't believe what she saw. Right in the center were several baby skunks. Edith screamed at the top of her lungs, "Children, run!" Then the funniest thing happened. Each kid grabbed a skunk and ran! Mom's biggest problems were just beginning. Can you imagine that?

Worry. Discouragement. Depression. Exhaustion. Frustration. Letdown. Everybody faces these dragons plenty often. Sometimes the dragon wins!

That reminds me of a poster a friend showed me about a year ago. I thought it had a great message. It showed a knight in his armor. He looked half dead. His armor was blackened by fire. The feathering on his helmet was singed off. His jousting spear was snapped in two. His shoulders were slumped, and his face held the sad look of defeat.

Standing opposite him was the dragon with which he had just done battle. A huge, ugly grin shone on his face. With smoke still rising from his nostrils, he appeared to be pounding his tail on the ground in pride. The caption beneath simply said, "Some days the dragon wins."

Ever felt like that knight? Guess what? You will again. But don't let that get you down. Instead, get hold of the promise that Psalm 91:1 offers. Find that "shelter." Step into God's shadow. Catch some shade. Then you'll be ready to get back into the challenge of life. Because some days the dragon *loses*.

> Did we in our own strength confide,
> Our striving would be losing;
> Were not the right Man on our side,
> The man of God's own choosing.
> Dost ask who that may be?
> Christ Jesus, it is He;
> Lord Sabaoth His name,
> From age to age the same,
> And He must win the battle.
> —*Martin Luther*

David, our psalmist, had numerous run-ins with "dragons." One time that stands out in my memory was at a town called Ziklag. How would you like to have a place with a name like that for a hometown? David and his army came home to Ziklag and found it burned to the ground. The women and children had been kidnapped. The Bible says that the men "wept aloud until they had no strength left to weep." The dragon, depression, had set in. But 1 Samuel 30:6 adds that "David found strength in the Lord his God." That's the only way to become a dragon-slayer.

Depression can still be a very real problem, especially in our complex world. Frank Minirth and Paul Meier see the pain of depression regularly. They are psychiatrists. In their book *Happiness Is a Choice,* they point out some tough truths:

> Depression is a devastating illness that effects the total being—physically, emotionally, and spiritually. The emotional pain of depression is more severe than the physical pain of a broken leg. Unlike a broken leg, however, the pains of depression come on much more gradually. Many men and women are currently suffering from numerous symptoms of depression without even realizing that they suffer from depression rather than from some purely physical illness.

When frustrations, failures and discouragements swarm around us like so many bumble bees and leave their stingers heart-deep, the hurt is hard to cope with. The psalms can be a great hideout. They leave us to a private shelter. A spiritual fallout cellar.

What did David mean when he said, "He who dwells in the *shelter* of the Most High"? A shelter is a place of protection. It is a place of security. We can go there when the dragon is winning.

Would you like a road map to that shelter? It's a secret place. Only a few find it, because only a few look for it. And it's quiet there. Once you experience it, you will want to go back over and over. Ready to look for it?

First of all, you begin by going alone. Later on, when you are able to get there easily, you can show others the way. But for now begin alone. Take your Bible with you. Take a pencil and a notebook.

The place itself can be almost anywhere. Your room. In the backyard under an oak tree. Down by a creek. Wherever you can be by yourself for a few minutes. Go there. Sit down. Get comfortable.

Then open your Bible to a Psalm, or Proverb, or to the Gospels, or to any Scripture you like. Close your eyes and tell God just what's on your heart. He's quite familiar with dragons, especially that old dragon—Satan!

Read for a while. Rest for a while. Jot down a couple of sentences in your notebook about what you read. This is what some people call devotions, or quiet time. David called it shelter. You don't need to stay there for long. But don't be in a hurry to leave, either.

The most wonderful thing happens there. A great shadow rolls overhead. No, not a dark cloud. Not the shade of a tree. Not an eclipse. Spiritual shade, that's it! God overshadows all the despair with love and comfort. He sends you away with new strength. For all your Ziklags, God sends a shadow of help, if you will only take the time to look for it and rest in it.

It would be nice if I could tell you that trouble never comes, that you will never get depressed. It would be even better if I could say that the devil will never bother you, that temptation will never happen again. Of course, that would be silly. We both know the score. However, we can thank God for his comforting shadow during these times.

> How desolate my life would be,
> How dark and drear my nights and days,
> If Jesus' face I did not see
> To brighten all earth's weary ways.
> I'm overshadowed by His mighty love,
> Love eternal, changeless, pure
> Overshadowed by His mighty love,
> Rest is mine, serene, secure.
>
> —*H. A. Ironside*

Now, if you ever run into a "stinking" mess like Edith's, you'll know what to do. Find a shadow.

# 12 Forgiven!

## *Water Under the Bridge*

*Blessed is he whose transgressions are forgiven, whose sins
are covered (Ps. 32:1).*

Copernicus was a famous mathematician. Centuries ago,
his studies and calculations changed man's understanding of the
universe. What would a briliant man like that want carved on his
tombstone? A geometrical theory? An unsolved calculus problem?
Some scholarly lines of poetry? How about an astronomical draw-
ing? No, none of those. These are the words he chose for his epitaph:

> I do not seek a kindness equal to that given to Paul. Nor do I ask
> the grace granted to Peter. But that forgiveness which Thou didst
> grant to the robber—that, earnestly I crave!

59

Forgiveness. Just like Jesus gave to the thief hanging on a cross next to his own. That's what so many people are looking for today. Every time somebody battles with guilt, he's looking for forgiveness. Whenever a person agonizes over the terrible pain that sin has brought, he's looking for forgiveness. It gives a freedom unlike any other feeling.

That people crave forgiveness can be seen in a lot of things. Here are a few:

**Psychological counseling is booming.** There are, of course, any number of things that people need help with. Many times the heaviest burden they carry is guilt. The hordes of patients who come to see counselors serve as a neon light. The first step to solving most of their problems is forgiveness. People like this need to get a load off their hearts more than just getting something off their chests. Mind you, that's not usually the whole solution, but it is a giant step in the right direction.

**Weird religious groups.** Wow! have you ever bumped into some of these kooks? They give me a serious case of the "willies" when I do. Especially the ones who shave and polish their heads. They all look alike—C3PO's and R2D2's. Spooky. There's another group that sends its members out to sell flowers on street corners. All of them have a faraway look in their eyes, as if they just walked out of Disneyland. Or, should I say, Dizzyland? Of course, this really is no joking matter. The reason why there are strange groups like these is their hunger for help—for forgiveness.

**Down-and-outers and up-and-outers.** Down-and-outers get drunk like bums on cheap whiskey, or high on bad drugs. Up-and-outers get drunk like bums on imported champagne, or high on finely cut cocaine. Whichever—they are sending out signals with their empty lifestyles. The signal is SOS: "I'm drowning in guilt. Please send forgiveness."

David, you remember, wrote most of the Psalms. He needed forgiveness a few times himself. His life was not always a Norman Rockwell painting of cuteness and purity. One time he stole a man's wife, committed adultery with her, and had her husband killed by staging an attack plan that left the good soldier out front all alone. Well, sin has its price tag; and David paid for that one his whole life long. But he still needed forgiveness. Psalm 51 was the prayer he prayed when the guilt of that awful sin began to eat at him. Here's part of it:

> Wash away all my iniquity and cleanse me from my sin. For I know my transgressions, and my sin is always before me. Against you, you only, have I sinned and done what is evil in your sight. . . . wash me, and I will be whiter than snow. . . . Create in me a pure heart, O God. . . .
>
> Ps. 51:2–4, 7, 10

That's serious praying. A far cry from the games some people play, thinking they can do whatever they please, then *tell* God to forgive them. Only to turn around and do the same things over again.

The good news about forgiveness is that it's free. It doesn't cost a dime. In fact, nobody has enough to buy it. God gives forgiveness to anybody who is willing to ask him—to those who are so fed up with what sin is doing to their lives that they are ready to cut it out.

Although forgiveness is free, it isn't cheap! It cost God a pretty penny. He bought forgiveness with a price that cannot be measured in dollars and cents. Jesus paid the bill for everybody when he died on the cross. His blood settled the account. So, if forgiveness is what you are after, you need to go to him. He's the owner of it. Don't worry; there is plenty to go around.

Sometimes we have to have his help in forgiving people who "did us wrong." Forgiving should be easier when we have been forgiven ourselves.

> Be kind and compassionate to one another, forgiving each other,
> just as in Christ God forgave you.
>
> Eph. 4:32

Comedian Bill Cosby tells a funny story from his childhood that shows the lengths we will go to "get even." One snowy afternoon he decided to ambush "Weird Harold" with a snowball. No slushy, gunky snowballs were allowed, so he had a nice fluffy one. When he was just about to cut loose on Harold, Pow!—out of nowhere came an extra-gunky snowball. The slush and goop were all over Cosby's face and ran down into his underwear!

When Cosby turned, he saw Junior Barnes, having a laughing fit. Cosby couldn't run fast enough to catch him. He sat down in a huge snowdrift and cried while the snow melted and soaked through his four pairs of corduroys.

From then on, Cosby was out to "get" Junior Barnes. He special-made a snowball and carved his name on it. Junior was hiding out, so Cosby put the snowball in the freezer for a better day. He waited until the next summer. It's now 104° in the shade and there isn't a snowball in sight.

By now, he and Junior are "fast friends." The trap is set. Cosby leaves Junior on the front porch while he goes into the house to get them a bottle of orange soda pop. When he gets to the freezer he really means to grab Junior's personalized snowball. Bummer of bummers! Cosby's mother has thrown the snowball away. That doesn't stop him. He marches outside to get his revenge. He spits on Junior Barnes!

I know that's a funny story, but we've all bumped into a Junior Barnes before. If we didn't feel like splitting, we felt like hitting. Instead we should be forgiving.

> Forgive and you will be forgiven.
>
> Luke 6:37

A very simple principle. No mathematical formulas are necessary to figure that out. Even Copernicus knew that.

# 13 Hope

## Blossom of Life

*But as for me, I will always have hope; I will praise you more and more (Ps. 71:14).*

**E**mily Dickinson's poetry has brought both joy and tears to thousands of poetry fans. She's an all-time favorite. A few of her lines describe "hope" in such a way as to make me stop and think, "Hmm . . . that's a neat way of saying it."

> "Hope" is the thing with feathers—
> That perches in the soul—
> And sings the tune without the words—
> And never stops—at all—

Hope is one of the untouchables. It's hard to get a handle on. I mean, what is it? Is it like a wish?

"I hope we get some rain."

"I hope the doctor bill isn't too high."

"I hope we don't run out of gas."

Or is it like a dream that may come true?

"It doesn't hurt to hope."

"I've got high hopes."

"Don't let your hopes get shattered."

Or is it like a last-ditch effort?

"You're our only hope, kid."

"I'm hoping against hope."

"All we can do now is hope."

It sort of gives the impression that when we're unsure of what will happen, we "hope." Or if we have no control over the outcome, we "hope." With it, we have something to look forward to. Without it, we're defeated.

Of course, hope doesn't just pop up on its own and say, "Well, here I am; you can be optimistic again." Something has to inspire hope. Something has to come along and give us reason to believe again. That's why the psalmist so often says, "Put your hope in God . . ." (Ps. 42:5). Because God is truly capable of making things happen.

As a matter of fact, it's needless to be hopeless. We have every reason to expect wonderful things to happen. For one, God is in the miracle business. It's no sweat for him to pull off a totally fabulous work. Miracles are tough stuff for us to perform, but God is the God of the miraculous.

Now and then God likes to put us in spots where we have to hope he will come though. (You see, hope and faith are blood brothers.) Take the children of Israel, for example. It was no small bind to be hanging out down by the Red Sea with nowhere else to go, while the Egyptians were on their way to create a massacre. That was all done according to plan, though. At the last minute, God put a heavenly karate chop on the waters. An exit to freedom for Israel, with new-found hope in hand. God was trying to teach them that he was reason enough to never give up. At any moment he could step in and change the ruins into rejoicing. That inspires hope!

Jesus was always a hope-bringer. Still is today. He had a friend named Lazarus. Lazarus up and died one day. That upset his sister Martha so much that she blamed Jesus. She said, "Lord, if you'd have been here, this wouldn't have happened." Then Jesus told her a deep truth—a truth that relates to hope. He said, "I am the resurrection and the life. He who believes in me will live, even though he dies; and whoever lives and believes in me will never die . . ." (John 11:25–26).

Outside of being a great promise for living in heaven someday, there is another nugget to be found in his words to huffy Martha. He was also hinting, in a way, that Martha had lost hope. He was saying, "Martha, live a resurrection life. Live as if you believe in something. Don't be such a fatalist!"

In case you are not familiar with the rest of the story, Jesus raised Lazarus up from the dead. Let me ask you: Do you think that would inspire hope for future dilemmas? You bet.

That the Lord is able to do above and beyond what we ask or think is only one reason to be full of hope. Here are a few others:

**God is on our side.** "God is our refuge and strength, an ever present help in trouble" (Ps. 46:1) is not a bland verse. God cares about what happens to us, and he is with us all the way. Abraham Lincoln pointed out, though, that it matters just as much that we be on God's side if we hope to have him on ours.

**Running away won't help.** "I said, 'Oh, that I had the wings of a dove! I would fly away and be at rest—I would flee far away and stay in the desert; I would hurry to my place of shelter, far from the tempest and storm'" (Ps. 55:6–8). Have you ever felt like running away from it all? That no matter how hard God was moving you in one direction, you didn't want to go that way? It can be tough to hope if the Lord's leading is different from what you had hoped.

Here's a poem about a fellow who wanted to run the opposite way from God's guidance. He thought that going God's way was hopeless.

> I said, "Let me walk in the fields."
>   He said, "No; walk in the town."
> I said, "There are no flowers there."
>   He said, "No flowers, but a crown."
> I said, "But the skies are black,
>   There is nothing but noise and din."
> And He wept as He sent me back;
>   "There is more," He said, "There is sin."
> I said, "But the air is thick
>   and the fogs are veiling the sun."
> He answered, "Yet souls are sick,
>   and souls in the dark undone."
> I said, "I shall miss the light,
>   and friends will miss me, they say."
> He answered, "Choose tonight
>   if I am to miss you, or they."
> I pleaded for time to be given.
>   He said, "Is it hard to decide?
> It will not seem hard in heaven
>   to have followed your Guide."
> I cast one look at the fields,
>   then set my face to the town;
> He said, "My child do you yield?
>   Will you leave the flowers for the crown?"
> Then into His hand went mine;
>   And into my heart came He;
> And I walk in the light divine,
>   The path I had feared to see.
>
>   —*Samuel Wilberforce*

That is hope. To face difficult situations clinging to God—instead of running away—is hope.

***We have much to look forward to.*** Colossians 1:27 ends with:

"Christ in you, the hope of glory." That's both the glory of eternity with the Lord and the glory of a full life. Christ is the Blessed Hope who fills life to overflowing.

What more could you hope for?

# 14 Fear

## *The Twilight Zone*

*The LORD is with me; I will not be afraid. What can man do to me? (Ps. 118:6).*

**W**ho hasn't heard the haunting words of Rod Serling in his once-popular, nightmarish television thriller?

You're traveling through another dimension. A dimension not only of sight and sound, but of mind. A journey into a wondrous land whose boundaries are that of imagination. At the signpost up ahead—your next stop—the twilight zone.

And then comes that crazy music.

Fear. He's the monster of emotions. He horrifies and terrifies, mesmerizes and paralyzes. He creeps in at the least expected times, making him all the more scary. He's everywhere:

| | |
|---|---|
| Fear of failure | Fear of being alone |
| Fear of crowds | Fear of rejection |
| Fear of death | Fear of heights |
| Fear of war | Fear of unemployment |
| Fear of marriage | Fear of crime |
| Fear of denists | Fear of the future |
| Fear of water | Fear of the dark |
| Fear of thunderstorms | Fear of airplanes |

President Franklin Roosevelt's words in his first inaugural address, March 4, 1933, say it best for us: "The only thing we have to fear is fear itself." Those are words to chew on. Fear on the loose in our emotions can destroy us.

Did you know that fear was the first negative feeling experienced by man? You know Adam, of Adam-and-Eve fame. Well, after Adam sinned he hid in the bushes. When God called to him, he answered by saying, "I heard you in the garden, and I was afraid because I was naked; so I hid" (Gen. 3:10).

That's panicky fear. I've felt that many times. When I was about ten years old, I hated going to bed. Because of the "sounds." I would just lie there, staring at the ceiling. Then I would hear them. Creaking floors. Whispering voices. A squeaky door. Footsteps. I used to think our house was haunted. Most of it was my imagination.

Catch that word—imagination. Because that's where fear acts out most of its shivers. It has been said that over 90 percent of our fears never happen. No matter how fierce they seem. No matter how gripping. Most of our fears are merely figments of our imagination.

So what? Does that make fear vanish? Hardly not. As long as we are able to think and feel, fear is going to be hanging around. That means we'll need some help in fighting back fright.

Our Psalm holds the key: "The Lord is with me." That's better than a burglar alarm, a large army, an indestructible fort, and a submachine gun rolled into one.

The disciples did not always know this. One time, when Jesus and the Twelve were taking an afternoon boat cruise, a furious storm came up. This was not your ordinary rain shower. The waves came roaring up over the boat, and for a while it looked as if they were making a pilot episode for *"Gilligan's Island."*

I get a kick out of the disciples. Sometimes they can be quite funny. They went into a frenzy. Screaming and dipping out water with coffee cans, they wanted to know where Jesus was. Where do you think he was? Asleep in the bottom of the boat. Twelve hearts beat with fury while Jesus took a nap.

"How can you sleep at a time like this?" they woke him up shouting. "There's a hurricane out here! What do you want us to do, drown? Save us!" (The exact story is in Matthew 8:23–27, since I am paraphrasing.)

Jesus sat up. Looked at them, disappointment flooding his eyes. Then he replied, "What's wrong with you guys? You don't have much faith in me. Why are you so afraid? Do you think I would just let the boat sink?"

He walked confidently out to the deck. Raised his hand. Said, "Be quiet." And the storm ended before an eye could blink. Completely calm. What a sight! One minute the storm raged in power; suddenly the waters were as placid as glass.

You should have heard those disciples talk as Jesus went to lie back down. They whispered, "What kind of man is this? Even the winds and waves obey him!"

Their problem was blindness. They failed to realize who was with them, of what he was capable. We can be just as blind at times. Although God is right there with us, we're frantic. Worried to death about how things are going to turn out. All along, he watches in disappointment at our lack of trust.

When God is with us, no one can be against us. Not and win. But when we give in to fears and doubts, the littlest things beat us down. It's like the old Scottish saying, "With God the most of the mosts is lighter than nothing, and without him the least of the leasts is heavier than my burden."

God's being with us can be the whole difference in how we look at things. If we yield to his presence and stay aware that he's there, confidence builds up in us. If we forget him and try to battle our spooky days alone, we'll end up petrified of life.

For example, take the group that was working on a crossword puzzle. One man asked, "What's a four-letter word for a strong inner response to difficulty?" One man answered, "Fear." A second person spoke up, "Love." Which of the two was most tuned in to God's presence?

John said, "There is no fear in love. But perfect love drives out fear, because fear has to do with punishment. The man who fears is not made perfect in love" (1 John 4:18). When you build a loving friendship with God, graduate, the fear quiets down like that storm did.

Paul said it this way, "For you did not receive a spirit that makes you a slave again to fear, but you received the Spirit of sonship. And by him we cry, 'Abba, Father'" (Rom. 8:15). Abba means "Daddy." God wants to give us the security a father gives, because he is our heavenly Daddy!

We should answer bravely, like Rostand's Cyrano de Bergerac did when he was told how outnumbered he was: "What! Odds of only a hundred to one?" When God is with us, we are never outnumbered. As Bob Jones, Sr., used to say, "God and you makes a majority."

Let that give you confidence the next time you take an uncharted course through the twilight zone.

71

# 15 Fate

## *Que Sera Sera?*

*Since you are my rock and my fortress, for the sake of your name lead and guide me (Ps. 31:3).*

Several years ago a freckled-face blonde by the name of Doris Day sang a popular tune:

> When I was just a little girl I asked my mother,
> "What will I be?
> Will I be pretty?
> Will I be rich?"
> Here's what she said to me.
> "Que sera sera!
> Whatever will be will be.

The future's not ours to see.
Que sera sera."

What do you think about that? Do you believe in "whatever will be will be"? Are we just puppets on a string, acting out a preset script? What role does luck play? Chance? Circumstances? Coincidence? Good questions.

God does have a will for our lives. He wants to lead and guide each of us. Too often the way some people go about finding God's will is through a "fleecelike" fate. They throw out a wild circumstance that will serve as a sign from heaven if it happens. Maybe you've heard about:

The college student who was seeking God's leading for a career. So he asked God for a "sign." The next day he bumped into a girl coming out of the library. She had a whole armload of books, but dropped only one. It was her zoology textbook. The young man took it as God's signal to become a zookeeper.

The high-school girl who couldn't decide if she should get married after graduation. She asked God to reveal her fate. When her car ran out of gas in front of a bridal shop, she "knew" it was God's will for her to get married.

The guy who dreamed he was locked in a concentration camp. The next day when the army recruiter called, he took it as a signal from heaven and joined right up.

Some people would say, "Well, that seems like good reasoning to me." Ridiculous! Others would say, "Pure coincidence." I don't think it was coincidence at all. In fact, a lot of things we think are strange coincidences are *nothing* at all. Funny circumstances can be just that. I'm afraid "fate" gets credit for many things that would usually go unnoticed. Sometimes we read too much into life, instead of taking it at face value.

But how about those circumstances? Does God ever bring about extraordinary circumstances to reveal his leading? I think so—

although circumstances alone should never be the sole deciding factor. God's Word, prayer, godly advice, and personal desire should also come into play.

Gideon is an example of a fellow who had one unusual circumstance after another point out the direction for him to take. He had two "fleece" prayers answered—both of which required genuine miracles (Judg. 6:36–40). First he prayed for his sheepskin to get soaked, but the ground to remain dry. It happened that night. The next night he prayed for the opposite. That, too, happened. So he obeyed God's call to lead Israel into battle.

Then Gideon had to assemble an army. Only the guys at a stream who lapped drinks by cupping water in their hands were to be chosen. He ended up with three hundred. Not exactly a multinational force or splendid war power.

The Midianites were thick as bugs when Gideon snuck up to scout out their camp. Just as he reached the outer limits of their army he overheard two Midianites talking.

One guy said, "I had the weirdest dream last night. In it this huge round roll of barley bread came crashing into the camp and knocked the tents down." Admit it. That is a strange dream!

The other guy, who had no way of knowing the unheard-of Gideon, said, "Oh, really? Well, that has to be Gideon, because God is going to use him to destroy us."

Figure the odds on Gideon's being there to hear that. Of all the places he could have scouted, that was the one. Before the night was over, Gideon's army destroyed the Midianites in the most outlandish battle strategy of history. If you don't believe me, read Judges 7.

God does use circumstances to direct us. However, we should never look at them as luck, chance, or fate. Philippians 2:13 says, "For it is God who works in you to will and to act according to his good purpose." God is busy in our lives, and we need to be alert to his guiding hand in a sensible way.

There is no such thing as luck or fate. "Providence" is the word for you. Providence is God providing the way. It's what I share in this

74

book's companion, *Proverbs for Graduates:* "Trust in the LORD with all your heart and lean not on your own understanding; in all your ways acknowledge him, *and he will make your paths straight*" (Prov. 3:5–6, italics mine).

Our mistake in seeking God's guidance is looking too far ahead, or in spending too much gloomy time looking back. We should concentrate on what the Lord has for us now. In *Knowing God's Will—and Doing It!,* J. Howard Grant hits on this:

> Can I know. . . of God's determined will for my life? Yes—after it has occurred! The remainder of your future is hidden from you until it happens. Your career, marriage partner, home location, grades in school, friends, sickness, accidents, honors, travels, income, retirement, etc., are all part of God's determined will but are not revealed to you ahead of time. . . . Don't worry about it and don't try to figure it out, because His ways are unfathomable.

Really, that's not bad advice. If you will just be open to God's leading at the moment, the "biggies" will be taken care of by God's grace. Enough Christians have horned in on their own lives and messed things up to show us that disobedience breeds disaster, and that obedience creates opportunity. Not fate! Taking things one step at a time is far more productive than trying to uncover the future with goofy fleeces of fate.

> He does not lead me year by year
> > Nor even day by day,
> But step by step my path unfolds;
> > My Lord directs my way.
>
> Tomorrow's plans I do not know,
> > I only know this minute;
> But He will say, "This is the way,
> > By faith now walk ye in it."
>
> And I am glad that it is so,

Today's enough to bear;
And when tomorrow comes, His grace
Shall far exceed its care.

What need to worry then, or fret?
The God who gave His Son
Holds all my moments in His hand
And gives them, one by one.
—*Barbara C. Ryberg*

As my good friend, author Dick Meier, has often said when helping me through the dark, confusing tunnels of life, "We don't have yesterday. And we can't be sure of tomorrow. But we do have now. Let us rejoice and be glad in it!"

Que sera sera? Hardly. Things don't fall out by chance. There is a purpose. Ask Gideon.

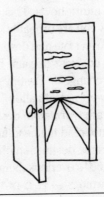

# 16 Destiny

## *Born to Become*

*My God, my God, why have you forsaken me? Why are you so far from saving me, so far from the words of my groaning? (Ps. 22:1).*

I read a quote recently that sent up my radar antenna. They were the words of Jean Paul Sartre:

> Man can will nothing unless he has first understood that he must count on no one but himself; that he is alone, abandoned on earth in the midst of his infinite responsibilities, without help, with no other aim than the one he sets himself, with no other destiny than the one he forges for himself on this earth.

Gobbledygook! We are not abandoned, and we are not alone. What's more, it's a tragic mistake to attempt "forging destiny" without God's direction in our lives. He is with us, and he has mapped out a highway of living for us all. He has a destiny for everyone, if we let him show us how to find it.

Interested? Millions of people are interested in the mysterious future, but not in God's blueprint. They read horoscopes, listen to psychics, fool with tarot cards and fortune-tellers, all in search of what the future holds. This is dim-witted living.

By now you are probably saying, "You talked about this in the last chapter. Aren't fate and destiny sort of the same thing?" Not exactly. Fate does not exist, because it says, "Hey! This was meant to be and you can't change it." Destiny says, "You're headed in a certain direction—toward a destination." The question is: Will you get there?

There are two *eternal* destinies. This is old news, but some people have not read the headlines. Heaven is the destination of some, and hell is the destination of others. Those facts are so well-known that we tend to overlook them, when we ought to be paying attention to the warnings—LIFE ENDS UP AHEAD!

Right now there could be dozens of graduates reading these words who haven't taken care of their eternal destiny. Who have never turned to Jesus Christ for salvation and forgiveness. Hell is not a red-decorated nightclub with a hot thermostatic reading. There's nothing funny about it! A big thought to remember is that once you reach your eternal destination you won't be leaving. It's the last stop. So be sure it's where you plan to stay.

Eternity is not the only destiny to think about, although it is—beyond a shadow of a doubt—the most important. You have a life to live. God has a purpose for you, goals for you, and a destination he wants you to reach. By graduating, you have already begun heading in that direction. From here on the choices you make will determine whether or not you reach your lifetime destiny. Will you accomplish what God has in mind for your life?

Stick with me now. This stuff is a little mind boggling, but it is also life changing. It can spill light onto your outlook. No one is happier than the one who knows what God wants for him or her and is heading straight in that direction.

Everybody is born for a reason. God wants you to become the individual he created you to be. That includes family, job, education, finances, whatever. Even Jesus had a destiny. Read our Psalm again. Jesus was born to die on the cross for our salvation. He knew that. But our Psalm cries out his pain. In spite of the agony, he did what God had set for him to do. He reached his destination.

Here's the thing. At any turn in life you might head in the wrong direction, which means you would not end up living out your life according to the blueprint. Your life would not be what God designed. You see, God doesn't force us to become something we don't want to be. But a person who keeps messing up and turning the wrong way shouldn't be surprised to end up at the wrong place. There's an old rhyme that drives this home:

> Sow a thought, and you reap an act;
> Sow an act, and you reap a habit;
> Sow a habit, and you reap a character;
> Sow a character, and you reap a destiny.

But is your life already preset? Is it prefabbed? No! That would be *"fate."* Your life is sketched, though. It's up to you to color between the lines. How? First of all, by settling your eternal destiny—receiving Christ into your life. Then, by obeying God's will. Day by day, it's becoming the unique person he made you to be. Filling that special spot in life created just for you. That's where you fit in. It's what makes your life count the most it can.

Now, the hard part. (This is meaty, isn't it?) You probably know very little about your destiny right now. Especially what you will become. But don't let that shake you up. You don't have to live tomorrow until it gets here. Just determine to become the best you can for God's glory.

There is one destiny that God wants us all to work toward in this life—becoming like Jesus (Rom. 8:29). Jesus is an example for us to imitate. This basic principle is the whole key to destiny. If we keep shooting for that goal—living life Jesus-style—the other parts of the future will fall into place.

Last question. If somebody is heading in the wrong direction, is it ever too late to turn around? That's a hard one. Although it's never too late to head the other way, spending too long on the wrong roads is a waste of time and of precious life. Getting real mixed up can cause major setbacks. It can keep you from reaching God's best.

The Book of Hebrews clues us in on following the right paths:

> Therefore, since we are surrounded by such a great cloud of witnesses, let us throw off everything that hinders and the sin that so easily entangles, and let us run with perseverance the race marked out for us. Let us fix our eyes on Jesus, the author and perfecter of our faith, who for the joy set before him endured the cross, scorning its shame, and sat down at the right hand of the throne of God. Consider him who endured such opposition from sinful men, so that you will not grow weary and lose heart.

Heb. 12:1–3

Hear that? Hang in there. Like Jesus did. In the face of cruelty and hate, he still reached his destiny. Since he did, we can reach ours. Even more, our eternal destiny can be known today!

Thy way, not mine, O Lord,
However dark it be;
Lead me by Thine own hand,
And choose the path for me.
I dare not chose my lot;
I would not if I might;
Choose Thou for me, my God,
So shall I walk aright.

The kingdom that I seek
Is Thine; so let the way

That leads to it be Thine,
   Else I must surely stray.
Hold Thou my cup of life;
   With joy or sorrow fill
As best to Thee may seem:
   Choose Thou my good and ill.

Choose Thou for me my friends,
   My sickness or my health;
Choose Thou my cares for me,
   My poverty or wealth.
Not mine, not mine the choice,
   In either great or small;
Be Thou my Guide, my Strength,
   My Wisdom, and my All.

               *—Horatius Bonar*

You have an appointment with destiny! Let God help you find him.

# 17 **Urgency**

## *Time in a Bottle*

*Wait for the LORD; be strong and take heart and wait for the LORD (Ps. 27:14).*

In the '70s a folksinger named Jim Croce sang a catchy ballad. What the song said about time is so true:

> If I could put time in a bottle,
> the first thing that I'd like to do,
> is to save every day 'til eternity ends,
> and then, I would spend them with you.
> Oh, there never seems to be enough time
> to do the things we want to do—
> If I could put time in a bottle.

Which phrase stands out most to you? The line that goes, "There never seems to be enough time to do the things we want to do," is right on target. No matter how fast we hurry, we keep running out of time.

American lifestyle calls everything urgent. Do it now. Rush, rush, rush! From stoplight to stoplight, from store to store, from morning to evening, from chore to chore—we are the busiest people in the world. We work hard and play even harder, and we only stop to sleep. Even then a good many of us will toss and turn all night, before we get up and repeat the same routine tomorrow.

When vacation comes we don't slow down; we shift into even higher gear. A couple of our friends just returned from vacation. What a marathon! They drove through six states, saw twenty major sights, covered over three thousand miles, spent over a thousand dollars, and all in one week. Boy, was it fun! But they're exhausted. Even vacation is celebrated with urgency.

James Sullivan knows all about this mad, mad, mad, mad world. He wrote a book entitled *The Frog Who Never Became a Prince*. It tells about his speed-of-light lifestyle that blazed him to success. About how the people he loves got left out of his life while he set a world-record pace for "busy living." About how his kids never saw him. About how his wife became a nervous wreck. About how his never-slow-down existence drove him to consider suicide.

Urgency does that. It wears the sharp edge off life. Eventually it causes every challenge to grow dull. Yesterday turns into the same old uneventful race with the clock. Tomorrow appears meaningless. Why? Because urgency is a thief. It steals the value of tasting life, instead of swallowing it whole.

e. e. cummings saw it. In his poem *"One Times One,"* he wrote: "Pity this busy monster, manunkind, not. Progress is a comfortable disease."

Busyness does make us monsters. It makes man unkind. Maybe e. e. has hit the nail dead center. Progress is a comfortable disease.

Maybe hurrying is a pain reliever for an empty life. We rush around to avoid seeing our real reflection.

"Wait!" is the word for the day. Slow down; you move too fast. Drink life in. Enjoy the day as it passes. Sponge up the splendor of living that floods over the dam of patience.

Patience? Yeah, patience. That's what waiting is all about. Learning to let God focus things for you before you snap the picture. It sure beats dashing through the years, clicking off memories, only to look back and wonder how it went so fast.

Patience means taking your time and letting God take his. Easily said, not so easily done. Especially now as you graduate. If you think high school was busy, wait until you see what's coming up next. Young adulthood is an all-out sprint. Patience is stopping for a breather.

Our "speed" trap has another catch. It teaches us to want things immediately. Like: a good job, a nice home, a new car, plenty of clothes, and so on. It lures us toward experiencing more and sooner. Another problem springs out of that—experimenting with sin when we get bored with "life as usual." That always spells disaster.

The cure for full-throttled living is waiting. That's a funny way of saying it, isn't it? You're thinking, "Wait? Wait for what? Do you mean just go sit down? Come on, be a little more specific. What does waiting mean?" Okay. So I owe you an explanation. Here goes:

***Waiting lets God catch up.*** Careful now; don't misunderstand me. I'm not saying that God is too slow. I'm saying that we're too fast. We get ahead of his plans. It would be better for us to be less urgent and more in unison with God's steps. Psalm 69:3 describes what it's like when we get miles out front: "I am worn out calling for help; my throat is parched. My eyes fail, looking for my God." He's way back there. It was John Wesley who said, "I'm always in haste, but never in a hurry." God doesn't want us to end up lazy bums, sitting around and doing nothing. He just wants us to walk in his footsteps. We need to paint Jeremiah's words over the front door to slip us a tiny reminder as we go out into the dog race. He said, "I know, O LORD, that a man's life is not his own; it is not for man to direct his steps" (Jer. 10:23). Anyone who forgets to wait patiently for God's timing is fast on the way to becoming a frog!

***Waiting sometimes means sitting still.*** You won't understand this until you get there, and then you'll point a finger in the air and whisper to yourself, "Ah! I see what you mean." Situations pop up occasionally that are downright dumbfounding. They knock you flat. During these times, sitting still is about the best we can muster up. One more step brings another dose of confusion. Waiting helps sift out the problem for a solution. Milton said, "They also serve who only stand and wait." This standstill doesn't last forever. It's a time of soul-searching. Psalm 37:7 makes this clear: "Be still before the Lord"; and Psalm 46:10 adds "Be still, and know that I am God."

***Waiting is a chance to get stronger.*** The word *wait* in the Old Testament has a root meaning of "twisting to make strong." The idea is that of a rope. The twists of hemp can become very powerful. We hang ourselves when we don't let the rope of life grow strong enough. Isaiah saw that waiting increases strength. His comforting words have helped hundreds: "Those who hope in [wait on] the LORD will renew their strength" (Isa. 40:31).

Life is too short to be wasted. Either by going too fast or by going too slowly. The graduate who learns that "the *stops* of a good man are ordered by the Lord," as well as the *steps,* is ready for a well-paced race. However, no matter how hard you try, you will never get time into a bottle.

# 18 Serenity
## *The Art of Unwinding*

*The LORD is my shepherd, I shall lack nothing. He makes me lie down in green pastures, he leads me beside quiet waters, he restores my soul (Ps. 23:1–3).*

An old Greek slogan for living goes like this: "You will break the bow if you keep it always bent."

Do you know what urgency (remember last chapter?) causes? Right—exhaustion! Americans can't resist becoming "-aholics" at whatever they do. There are workaholics, sportsaholics, churchaholics, televisionaholics, and even playaholics. What keeps us moving, anyway? Is it any wonder that burnout has become a hot topic, and that stress is a problem shared by millions? Many people would like to ease their stress and escape from being wound too tightly, if only they could squeeze it into their schedules.

You're entering a fantastic time of life! There are so many new activities and experiences to discover. The future is wide open. And the grind of high school is finally over. However, there will be plenty to put your schedule into the "overcommitted" category. Even at your youthful age, with enthusiasm brimming, it doesn't take long to feel like a tiny rubberband stretched to the limit, barely holding yourself together. Watch out in times like these for sudden snaps!

There's an art many of us are missing. It's called the art of unwinding. It means learning to let go, to stop strangle-holding life. Such a fierce grip chokes the daylight out of your life. Tim Hansel wrote a clever book about our stress-ridden world, entitled *When I Relax, I Feel Guilty*. In it he touches on serenity, on unwinding.

> Slow me down, Lord.
> Ease the pounding of my heart by the quieting of my mind.
> Steady my hurried pace with a vision of the eternal reach of time.
> Give me, amid the confusion of the day, the calmness of the everlasting hills.
> Break the tensions of my nerves and muscles with the soothing music of the singing streams that live in my memory.
> Teach me the art of taking minute vacations—of slowing down to look at a flower, to chat with a friend, to pat a dog, to smile at a child, to read a few lines from a good book.
> Slow me down, Lord, and inspire me to send my roots deep into the soil of life's enduring values, that I may grow toward my greater destiny.
> Remind me each day that the race is not always to the swift; that there is more to life than increasing its speed.
> Let me look upward to the towering oak and know that it grew great and strong because it grew slowly and well.

The Twenty-third Psalm is the dearest of psalms, the favorite of thousands. Its lines are profoundly poetic and yet possess childlike simplicity. There's a certain tenderness about its language. It is serene, and it inspires serenity. Just in those first three verses, the art of unwinding unfolds. The rhapsody of those words calms us each time we hear them. Step into the Shepherd's pasture and unwind.

*Feel God's perfect peace.* The quiet waters. In our hustle-bustle world, it's no wonder this Psalm touches a soft spot. We long for peace and quiet. But what *is* peace? We've been zooming around so much that most of us have not the slightest idea of what it is, how to have it, where it comes from, or what it feels like.

For one thing, it isn't an escape. It isn't artificial. You can't get it from a bottle, from pills, from a guru, or from having "everything." It can't be bought. Crowds can't give it, and neither can being alone. Manufactured peace never lasts. It gradually fades to black. Only authentic peace endures. In spite of pain, disappointment, fatigue, and loss, this peace sticks like glue.

Jesus, and only Jesus, gives it. If you want the "quiet waters" kind of peace to flow in your heart and mind, then you'll have to chat with Jesus. He will say, "Peace I leave with you; my peace I give you. I do not give to you as the world gives. Do not let your hearts be troubled and do not be afraid" (John 14:27). ". . . in me you may have peace. In this world you will have trouble. But take heart! I have overcome the world" (John 16:33). That's pretty plain, don't you think?

"Great," you say, "but what is this peace like? How will I know when I have it?" Don't get the wrong idea. Peace is not the absence of conflict, but the ability to cope with it. Peace is the inner confidence that God will never let you down. That he always has his finger on the situation. When peace reaches this peak, it cannot be described. Philippians 4:7 says, "And the peace of God, which transcends all understanding, will guard your hearts and your minds in Christ Jesus." Real, lasting peace is hard to explain, but you will know when you have it. It's unmistakable.

> Drop thy still dews of quietness,
> Till all our strivings cease;

Take from the souls our strain and stress;
  And let our ordered lives confess
The beauty of thy peace.
            —*John Greenleaf Whittier*

Someone has said, "Great people are not affected by each puff of wind that blows ill. Like great ships, they sail serenely, on, in a calm sea or a great tempest." In other words, even when the waters aren't quiet on the outside, they can be on the inside.

***Enjoy God's roomy rest.*** Ever feel boxed-in? Cramped? Bottled-up inside? Here's an invitation to the wide-open spaces of green acres. Lie down in soft pastures. Enjoy the stillness of a hidden meadow deep in your soul.

This will be a great help when the time comes for college to begin; or when that big job interview looms; or when you go out on your own for the first time. It might be impossible to sleep at night, unless you find this rest.

Psalm 62:1 makes an important discovery. Stash it in your memory. "My soul finds rest in God alone. . . ." The rest in your days comes when you rest in his ways. Relax the bow's tension before it breaks.

***Accept God's sweet security.*** Serenity flees from worrywarts. Let these words sink in, "The Lord is my shepherd, I shall lack nothing." Repeat them to yourself silently, over and over again until you believe them.

Don't be guilty of being like the anonymous guy in this little poem:

Before his life was hardly begun,
  He had died a thousand deaths, save one;
He was betrayed by a wife he never married,
  He was shot by a gun he never carried;
He was killed in battles he never fought,
  He died with disease he never caught.

He flunked out in classes he never started,
    Was swallowed in Red Sea he never parted;
He starved when his stomach and pantry were filled,
    Was worried and restless when his spirits were stilled,
So, when *real troubles* came along his way,
    He had little courage to face that day.

Insecurity is sneaky. But deadly! Once it latches on, it's hard to shake. Like a bloodsucking tick, it drinks away your serenity. Insecurity carries us out into a sea of defeat, like a subtle current. What we need is an anchor. Anchors hold us in place. Anchors are security. Our anchor is Jesus.

Take a dip into the serene. Unwind. Before you come unglued.

# 19 Loneliness

## *Is Anyone Out There?*

*You have taken my companions and loved ones from me; the darkness is my closest friend (Ps. 88:18).*

Eleanor Rigby. She wasn't a person, but a song. She was the creation of the Beatles rock group. The song mentions the sermons of Father McKenzie—the sermons that no one will hear because no one comes near. It's an unsettling tune with a sarcastic tone.

"All the lonely people" is the nagging, repetitious punch line. "Wake up!" the Beatles seem to be saying, "the world's full of people desperate for love, hungry for attention, wishing someone would care. And all the Father McKenzie's are blowing it!"

"Eleanor Rigby" was meant to be a putdown. The song was a shot at Christianity for being unable to help all the lonely people. Well, personally, I think the Beatles were out to lunch. They saw Christianity as the organized church, which does fail sometimes because its people are imperfect. But Christianity is really a person—Jesus Christ. He never fails those who come to him. He is the cure for the "lonelies."

Loneliness comes in through any door of life where you'll let it. Through the door of dating—not having a boyfriend or girlfriend, someone to call your own. Through the door of change—missing everything you're familiar with, such as when you go away to college or move out on your own. Through the door of friends, when you don't have anyone to turn to. Through the door of death, when you lose someone you need and love. Through the door of solitude—being cooped up all alone. That's the feeling you get when there's nothing to do and nobody around. Through the door of crowdedness—becoming a mere number, a statistic in the huddled masses. Through the door of emptiness—being homesick for something more out of life. Through the door of nostalgia—looking back at what you used to be.

In fact, graduation itself provokes a certain kind of loneliness. A loneliness for yesterday. Growing up is fun and challenging and inescapable and sometimes lonely. Glancing back, you probably cannot help but miss some of the old things that you've outgrown. Sometimes when we see our present selves, we wish we could turn back the clock for just a little while.

> Across the fields of yesterday
> He sometimes comes to me
> A little lad just back from play
> The boy I used to be.
>
> He smiles at me so wistfully
> When once he's crept within
> It is as though he'd hoped to see
> The man I might have been.
>
> —Anonymous

Everybody has felt lonely. Even famous Bible characters had their moments in solitary confinement. Take Moses. For forty years he traipsed around in the wilderness with well over a million people who often hated him. His job of leadership was very lonely. Most leadership is.

How about Elijah? A no-account woman named Jezebel was killing the prophets. Believe me, they were dropping like flies. That sort of spooked Elijah. Since he wasn't too excited about becoming her next shish kebab, he ran into the mountains and hid in a cave. There's nothing wrong with self-preservation, except that God didn't want Elijah in a cave. He wanted him to face Jezebel.

Let's pick up with the scene in 1 Kings 19:12–14, because it is perfect just as it reads:

> . . . And after the fire came a gentle whisper. When Elijah heard it, he pulled his cloak over his face and went out and stood at the mouth of the cave.
> Then a voice said to him, "What are you doing here, Elijah?"
> He replied, "I have been very zealous for the LORD God Almighty. The Israelites have rejected your covenant, broken down your altars, and put your prophets to death with the sword. I am the only one left, and now they are trying to kill me too."

Does that sound like a lonely man? Absolutely! Did you hear what he said? *I am the only one left.* But he wasn't. There were actually seven thousand left. Why did he feel that way? Self-pity. Sometimes loneliness is caused by self-pity.

Take a look again at our Psalm. No companions and loved ones. Darkness as a best friend. Sounds gloomy. And the tone of the words isn't good either. The psalmist appears to be blaming God for his loneliness. That only brings deeper solitude.

Then there was Peter. Remember when he denied Jesus? He cursed and said he'd never heard of Jesus. Afterwards he went out and cried all night long. Disobedience brings an emptiness, a strange loneliness.

Of course, Jesus himself felt alone as he hung on the cross. His disciples fled, and the jeering mob made jokes about him. His loneliness came from rejection. Just like leadership, self-pity, loss, and sin, rejection has a way of making us feel like aliens—friendless.

In 1942 a country-western singer crooned a ballad about loneliness. Since he lived a sad, heartbroken life, some say that Hank Williams sang about himself. The words are haunting. They portray the pain of feeling alone:

> Hear that lonesome whippoorwill?
> He sounds too blue to fly.
> The midnight train is whining low,
> I'm so lonesome, I could cry.

Loneliness is a desperate feeling. It eats at your insides and bores a hole through your heart. It makes you tired, but keeps you awake. It robs you of happiness. It makes you think there's no hope for tomorrow, that you'll never get over feeling so down.

There is a cure. Works every time. Loneliness is the absence of a meaningful relationship. God is always there to provide the friendship and companionship we need. Listen to some of these promises:

God has said, *"Never will I leave you; never will I forsake you"* (Heb. 13:5).

Jesus said, *"And surely I will be with you always, to the very end of the age"* (Matt. 28:20).

The Lord God said, *"It is not good for man to be alone. . ."* (Gen. 2:18)

Jesus said, *"I will not leave you as orphans. . ."* (John 14:18).

The Lord Jesus Christ wants to chase away the blues. He says, "Here I am! I stand at the door and knock. If anyone hears my voice and opens the door, I will come in and eat with him, and he with me"

(Rev. 3:20). Jesus wants to build a friendship, one where you feel free to come to him anytime the anguish of not having anyone sets in.

Proverbs 18:24 puts the icing on the cake. It says, "There is a friend who sticks closer than a brother." That's Jesus. He never gives us the silent treatment. He never gets too busy. He's always there. Always caring, always understanding. Always touched by our hurt and moved by our pleas for help.

Eleanor Rigby should have met him. And so should everyone who ever feels lonesome enough to cry.

# 20 **Brokenness**

## *Cast of Thousands*

*The LORD is close to the brokenhearted and saves those who are crushed in spirit (Ps. 34:18).*

Tennyson's "In Memoriam" speaks for the hordes who have felt heartbreak and heartache:

> That loss is common would not make
> My own less bitter, rather more:
> Too common! Never morning wore
> To evening, but some heart did break.

This chapter is not about broken bones, but about broken hearts. That's something no plaster cast can help. The hard-to-mend broken heart requires a different cast for healing. A cast made to fit thousands. Because if brokenness were a Broadway play, it would have thousands in its cast.

Brokenness comes in many forms. Here are only a handful of fractures felt in our world every day:

There sits a single girl. She hates being single. But the prospects of marriage aren't good. No takers. She fears being an old maid. The mirror smirks at her, telling her she's a nobody—unwanted property.

Yonder goes a man whose heart needs stitches. His wife just divorced him. Took both children. She loves another man. She's been having an affair since long before the divorce. Now he lives in a one-bedroom apartment. One broken heart for sale.

In stunned silence sit two parents. They represent the thousands who share their private nightmare. In a flash they lost a child. It happens every day. A car accident. A drug overdose. A killing. A kidnapping. An incurable disease. No matter, because nothing makes a child's life seem long enough. Memories are hard to turn to.

She can't figure out why her fiancé broke things off. Everything was going perfectly. Now the relationship is over. She hides it well, but last night she cried until there were no more tears left.

Being paralyzed isn't easy. Especially when you used to be a good athlete. That guy over there faces a brokenness most people never understand.

Him? Lost his job. With a family to feed and bills to pay, he's sorely troubled.

The blind, the deaf, the orphaned, the childless, the grieving, the handicapped, and the list goes on—people whose lives seem shattered, whose dreams seem unfulfilled.

We've all experienced this type of suffering in one way or another. Martha Snell Nicholson's poem "Guests" is for us:

Pain knocked upon my door and said
　　That she had come to stay,
And though I would not welcome her
　　But bade her go away,

　　She entered in.
Like my own shade
She followed after me,
And from her stabbing, stinging sword
　　No moment was I free.

And then one day another knocked
　　Most gently at my door.
I cried, "No, Pain is living here,
　　There is not room for more."

And then I heard His tender voice,
　　"'Tis I, be not afraid."
And from the day he entered in,
　　The difference it made!

***Brokenness directs us to Christ.*** He is the healer. By miracle power, he is able to touch our bleeding wounds and make them well. It's what he meant when he preached from Isaiah:

> The Spirit of the Sovereign LORD is on me, because the Lord has anointed me to preach good news to the poor. He has sent me to bind up the brokenhearted, to proclaim freedom for the captives and release for the prisoners, to proclaim the year of the LORD's favor and the day of vengeance of our God, to comfort all who mourn, and provide for those who grieve in Zion—to bestow on them a crown of beauty instead of ashes, the oil of gladness instead of mourning, and a garment of praise instead of a spirit of despair . . . (Isa. 61:1–3 and Luke 4:18).

Jesus was broken. On Calvary, he suffered shame and agony. He wept. He prayed. He could have come down, if he had wanted to. He could have called zillions of angels to the rescue, but he didn't. He died. However, so that he could heal all our brokenness, he came back to life three days later! Jesus has proved his love and his power to mend broken hearts.

***Brokenness also develops us in Christ.*** Humility is honed here. The jagged edges of pride are the first things broken. Some people are so stubborn that they would never turn to the Lord, unless some sort of burden came their way. Trials break our willfulness. Adversity makes us ready to grow. Psalm 51:17 backs me up on that 100 percent. "The sacrifices of God are a broken spirit; a broken and contrite heart, O God, you will not despise."

Don't get me wrong. God doesn't sit around whipping up tragedies for kicks. Our God is tenderhearted. He isn't clapping his hands while people live in torment. He holds his arms open wide, and with our pride gone, it's easier to run to him.

Compassion is constructed during this time. We start noticing the hurts of others. When someone else cries, we can sympathize better. We learn to be more caring through our ordeals. This is also when patience is patented. Anybody who can endure heartbreak and setback can deal with life's little scratches.

Our wounds gradually turn into scars of humility, compassion, and patience. Although scars don't hurt, the memories still do. Scars are reminders. Jesus has scars. They are the only man-made things in heaven. He got them from reaching out to love us. Look at his hands, his feet, and his side, not to mention his heart. Now look at yourself by comparison. How about your scars?

> Hast thou no scar?
> No hidden scar on foot, or side, or hand?
> I hear thee sung as mighty in the land,
> I hear them hail thy bright ascendant star,
> Hast thou no scar?
>
> Hast thou no wound?
> Yet I was wounded by the archers, spent,

Leaned Me against a tree to die; and rent
By ravening beasts that compassed Me, I swooned:
Hast thou no wound?

No wound, no scar?
Yet, as the Master shall thy servant be,
And, pierced are the feet that follow Me;
But thine are whole: can he have followed far
Who has no wound nor scar?

—*Amy Carmichael*

I only have a single word to add to those solemn lines—*Selah!*

Can I toss out one last thought? Thanks, because it has colossal importance. . . .

**Brokenness defeats us without Christ.** Proverbs 17:22 tells us that "a crushed spirit dries up the bones." It takes time to dry anything, but a broken heart will parch you faster than a hair dryer can get the wet out. Unless! Unless you reach out to Jesus. He puts the salve on. That's why he is called the Balm of Gilead.

And God who gives beginnings
    Gives the end;
A place for broken things
    Too broke to mend.

The only cure for a broken heart is to be broken enough to say, "Lord, I'm broken! Will you put me back together again?" Then he turns the suffering into a scar.

# 21 | Prayer

## 911 Emergency

*In return for my friendship they accuse me, but I am a man of prayer (Ps. 109:4).*

I'd like to ask you a highly personal question. How's your prayer life? Wait a minute. Don't answer too quickly. Make sure nobody else is around, because this isn't meant to embarrass you. Be honest. How's your prayer life?

It's been said that if you wanted to humble someone, you should ask about his or her praying. In no area do we fail as much as this one. While most of us would agree that praying is important, we would also have to admit that our own prayer lives have lots of ups and downs. With the "downs" holding a whopping lead.

Here's where the Psalms come to the rescue. Did you know that most of the Psalms are actually prayers? They are. Read a couple of them straight through. They talk directly to God. They ask him to listen. They cry out for help. We can learn bunches about praying by just snooping through the Psalms.

Maybe you look upon prayer as something for the "really religious" people. That's because praying is purely spiritual and has nothing to do with knowledge. Or ability. Or talent. Or popularity. Everybody is on the same turf when it comes to praying. It means getting down to business. It means being humble, instead of acting "in control." It means having a serious, personal relationship with Jesus Christ. Prayer is not very appealing to people who like to think they can figure things out for themselves.

Some people don't pray because they don't know how. Even Jesus' disciples didn't know how. They said, "Lord, we'd sure like to learn how to pray. Could you teach us?" Then Jesus prayed the Lord's Prayer, but not so that everybody would run around repeating it. The Lord's Prayer was a model, an example to pattern prayers after. Like what? Look at Matthew 6:9–13. Here are a few of the lessons to be learned from the Lord's Prayer:

| Lord's Prayer | Lesson |
|---|---|
| Hallowed be your name | Pray with respect |
| Your will be done | Pray for God's will in your situation |
| Give us our daily bread | Pray for basic needs |
| Forgive us our debts | Pray for forgiveness regularly |
| Deliver us from evil | Pray for victory over temptation |

Outside of those plain instructions, prayer is simply talking to God. No fancy language is needed. Prayer is not a monologue. It's a dialogue. You don't have to be "Joe Christian" or super godly to pray. If Jesus is your Savior, you can talk to the Lord anywhere, at any time. And he promises to listen. You can't beat that deal.

Some people have given up on prayer. They don't think it does any good. Most of the time we're in a hurry and can't understand why God isn't more understanding. Why doesn't *he* ever get in a hurry? Probably the best thing to remember when God seems slow is that his ways are perfect. Since God does not make mistakes, we should relax and keep praying.

Prayer may not always change things, but it always changes *us*. It changes our attitude, outlook, and approach. As we open up to God, unashamed and unafraid, he does something neat. He takes a heavenly hammer and chisel and makes us into better people—often by answering our prayers in ways we never expected.

> I asked God for strength, that I might achieve,
> I was made weak, that I might learn humbly to obey.
> I asked for health, that I might do greater things,
> I was given infirmity, that I might do better things.
> I asked for riches, that I might be happy,
> I was given poverty, that I might be wise.
> I asked for power, that I might have the praise of men,
> I was given weakness, that I might feel the need of God.
> I asked for all things, that I might enjoy life,
> I was given life, that I might enjoy all things.
> I got nothing that I asked for—but everything I had hoped for,
> Almost despite myself, my spoken prayers were answered.
> I am among all men most richly blessed.

Psalm 91:15 is a fantastic promise. It says: "He will call upon me, and I will answer him; I will be with him in trouble, I will deliver him and honor him." Isaiah 65:24 is like it: "Before they call I will answer; while they are still speaking I will hear." God wants us to pray. He's eager for us to do it and is even more eager to help us. Whatever the need. Whatever the prayer.

There are different kinds of prayers. Pick out the one you need right now. Then try it. See what kinds of changes take place. Let God surprise you!

***Chatting.*** This is a fun way to pray, like little friendship talks with the Lord. No major problems to discuss. No gargantuan requests.

Just conversation. It provides a good opportunity to share your day's plans with God and ask for his help and guidance. If something is bothering you, this is a perfect time to tell the Lord about it. Chatting with the Lord builds strong ties. And it makes turning to him in the tough times easier.

*Wishing.* Sound strange? It isn't. God is not a dummy. You can't hide anything from him. He knows you have secret dreams and desires. Some of them are selfish. He knows that. Some of them are wrong for you. He knows that, too. But he never minds listening. In fact, God can work through your wishing. If you want the right things, God sometimes brings them into your life—slowly, so as not to ruin you. Sound too good to be true? Psalm 37:4 says, "Delight yourself in the LORD and he will give you the desires of your heart." Just don't overlook the first part of that verse.

*Emergency.* This is the 911 call to heaven. Code blue. "Emergency, God! Please come quick!" Crisis is a popular time to cry for help. Unfortunately, it's the only time some people pray. As long as life glides smoothly along, they don't phone heaven for a thing. Not even to say "Hi!" However, God does not only want to help in the emergencies of life; he also wants to be a part of the whole expanse of life. In other words, don't just heat up the 911 hotline to heaven.

*Desperation.* When a crash landing is unavoidable, all that's left is desperation. Too often these prayers come after all the damage has been done. Now the request is, "Daddy, fix it." Life is not a toy. It is fragile. When broken, repairs bring pain. There are no quick fixes, not even with God. Don't wait until you are desperate to start praying. Let God be the Pilot, and you'll miss the crashes of life.

Is your prayer life hurting? Give a call right now? Just say, "Lord, it's me. Forgive me for not calling sooner." You won't even get a bill for it at the end of the month.

## 22 Glory

### Somewhere over the Rainbow

*And in his temple all cry, "Glory!" (Ps. 29:9)*

**I**n 1939 one of the all-time classic movies was made—*The Wizard of Oz*. You've seen it—Dorothy, the Tin Man, the Scarecrow, the Lion, the yellow brick road, the witches, and all that—haven't you? Well, then, you'll recognize these words:

> Somewhere over the rainbow
> Bluebirds fly.
> Birds fly over the rainbow—
> Why, then Oh, why can't I?

The sky has always fascinated mankind. We watch the birds fly up there, and we imitate them in huge airliners. We look at the stars and name them. We are curious about space, and we send astronauts in spaceships up there on special missions. But our curiosity never diminishes. Maybe it's because of a craving deep inside us that says there's something at the end of this universe—Someone! And if Someone, then someplace. A unique place. What the Bible calls heaven.

Heaven is heaven because God is there. He makes it a place of beauty. A place of awe. A place of majesty. A place of celebration. A place of glory. We know so little about glory.

An old saying goes, "Don't be so heavenly-minded that you're of no earthly good." That's good advice. We shouldn't walk around with our head up in the clouds. Life needs careful attention. However, it's just as important not to be so earthly-minded that we are of no heavenly good.

The apostle Paul said it this way, ". . . set your hearts on things above, where Christ is seated at the right hand of God. Set your minds on things above, not on earthly things. When Christ, who is your life, appears, then you also will appear with him in glory" (Col. 3:1–2,4).

Do you know what I get from that? That Paul wanted us to concentrate on God's glory instead of earthly glory. Because as we let thoughts of heaven cascade into our minds like an overflowing waterfall, it will make us a channel of blessing down here.

Have you ever sat down and thought about heaven? Not just fleeting thoughts. But serious ones. Ever wonder what it looks like? What are people doing up there? Do they just sit around and act holy? Do they play basketball? What do they eat? Is there pizza in heaven? (I couldn't make it without pizza.) What kind of music do they have? Angels flying around with harps? What do they talk about? Old high-school memories?

Let's take a peek, want to? Since we can't see it with a telescope, let's use God's looking glass—the Bible. But let's not make golden streets, crystal sidewalks, and tree-of-life fruit trees the big deal. Let's look closer at what makes it "Glory!"

**God is there.** "That Jesus is there is what makes it heaven for me," says the songwriter. In Isaiah 66:1, God says, "Heaven is my throne. . . ." I can't describe that. Wish I could. But the Bible says God's presence is breathtaking. Read Revelation 21:23: "The city does not need the sun or the moon to shine on it, for the glory of God gives it light, and the Lamb is its lamp." Amazing! Does that mean that God will be too bright to look at? I don't think so. Somehow his radiance will be strong enough to light all of heaven and yet not blind our eyes in any way. That is glory!

**Christian family and friends are there.** When people who have trusted in Jesus Christ die, they go to heaven. The Bible says that to be absent from the body is to be at home with the Lord (2 Cor. 5:8). So, hoping we will see Christian family members and friends is not like a wish, or a dream come true. Someone once asked a preacher, "Well, do you think we will recognize each other in heaven? Do you think we'll still know each other?" He laughed and answered, "Sure! You don't think we'll be stupider up there than we are down here, do you?" And we read: "Now we see but a poor reflection; then we shall see face to face. Now I know in part; then I shall know fully, even as I am fully known" (1 Cor. 13:12). Our relationships in heaven will be better. Because we will live in a new dimension.

**There is no sin there.** Revelation 21:27 teaches: "Nothing impure will ever enter it. . . ." Imagine that. We won't have to worry about temptation, or failure, or disappointing the Lord. The morning newspaper—*The Heaven Times*—won't carry a single story about evil. We won't read about rape, theft, murder, child abuse, nuclear war, racism, organized crime, or beatings. And we will never again have to worry about being victims.

**There is no suffering there.** I love this part. We can do a tap dance of joy over this one: "He will wipe every tear from their eyes.

There will be no more death or mourning or crying or pain, for the old order of things has passed away" (Rev. 21:4). Wow! Depression bites the dust forever. No more broken hearts or broken bones. Everything that makes earth a miserable, painful place to live in is dead. Even death dies!

> There's no disappointment in heaven,
> No weariness, sorrow or pain,
> No hearts that are bleeding and broken,
> No song with a minor refrain.
> The clouds of our earthly horizon
> Will never appear in the sky,
> For all will be sunshine and gladness,
> With never a sob nor a sigh.
>
> We'll never pay rent for our mansion,
> The taxes will never come due;
> Our garments will never grow threadbare,
> But always be fadeless and new;
> We'll never be hungry nor thirsty,
> Nor languish in poverty there,
> For all the rich bounties of heaven
> His sanctified children will share.
>
> There'll never be crepe on the doorknob,
> No funeral train in the sky;
> No graves on the hillsides of glory,
> For there we shall nevermore die.
> The old will be young there forever,
> Transformed in a moment of time;
> Immortal we'll stand in His likeness,
> The stars and the sun to outshine.
>
> I'm bound for that beautiful city
> My Lord has prepared for His own;
> Where all the redeemed of all ages
> Sing "Glory" around the white throne;
> Sometimes I grow homesick for heaven,
> And the glories I there shall behold:

What a joy that will be when my Saviour I see,
In that beautiful city of gold.

—*F. M. Lehman*

What more could be said? We'll fly through the air with the greatest of ease in a new body. A perfect body. We'll fly? Yes. In our heaven-designed body we'll make superman look like a slow boat to China.

Think about that the next time you see a rainbow.

# 23 Wonder

## *Escape from Fantasy Island*

*Let me understand the teaching of your precepts; then I will meditate on your wonders (Ps. 119:27).*

Some words of Albert Einstein inspire me. They make me want to adventure. They remind me that life is supposed to be exciting, not boring; amazing, not ordinary; awe-filled, not awful. Oh, well, back to Albert. He said, "The fairest thing we can experience is the mysterious. . . . He who knows it not, can no longer wonder, no longer feel amazement, is as good as dead, a snuffed out candle." Doesn't that make you want to live life on the cutting edge? It does me.

What is wonder? The dictionary calls it "feeling astonishment or admiration. To marvel as at a miracle. To experience something in a way far greater than previously known." Elizabeth Barrett Browning captures the idea with these words:

> Earth's crammed with heaven,
> And every common bush afire with God;
> But only he who sees, takes off his shoes.
> The rest sit round it and pluck blackberries.

Do you know what our trouble is? Nothing surprises us. We live in an age of such technology that we almost expect the unexpected. Videomania has robbed us of enjoying the greatest spectacular—life itself. Yet we are wowed by anything that appears on a screen.

Take computers. There seems no end to what computers can do. Just name something, and a computer can probably be put to use on it. I'm not against computers. They're here to stay. What irks me is that people get more excited about them than they do about God's marvels and miracles. What man makes eventually loses its sensationalism. God's stuff is just as breathtaking today as it was a hundred years ago, without changing or being updated once.

Videomania has not been the only robber of wonder-filled living. The almighty dollar has done its part. As someone has said, "Making a living has replaced making a life." It seems we'll never learn that the things we buy never hold a candle to the things that cannot be bought.

We've let life get plastic-coated. We trade amazement for amusement. Substitute thrills for happiness. Manufacture cheap experiences instead of seeking priceless moments that burn into our hearts the miracle of being alive. While we drift into fantasy, we are blind to the fantastic.

Do you know whose lives are filled with wonder? Little children. They're still surprisable. To their innocent eyes everything has a sparkle. They aren't wrapped up in the strange world of technology and empty pleasures that hypnotizes adults. God's world has their attention. A child can stare for an hour at an ant building an anthill

111

and be speechless. If a bird lands near a child, he is tender enough to believe that he can walk over and touch it, but only laughs when it flies away. Anything that blooms is a flower to a child. Children are awed by everything that God made and find it quite worth a celebration when they learn that God also made them. Jesus may have been driving home this point when he said, "I tell you the truth, unless you change and become like little children, you will never enter the kingdom of heaven" (Matt 18:3).

Maybe you've seen the TV show "Fantasy Island." It's about people who take a trip to an island to voyage into the impossible—their fantasies. Most of the time they learn that their wishful imaginings aren't everything they were cracked up to be. The artificial never tastes better than the actual.

You're probably thinking that to hear me tell it, life has no dull moments. Not true. The more we experience, the more prone we are to boredom. What I'm trying to get across is that challenges are everywhere. Plenty is left to be said. Lots left to be done. Some things can be felt over and over again without losing their magic. but if you do not search for these challenges, life will become a monotonous rut.

Above all, Jesus turns worthless ways into wonderful days. He caused gazes of astonishment during his earthly ministry. He still brings smiles of amazement to the lives of any who will follow him. As Isaiah said, his name is Wonderful (Isa. 9:6).

Jesus does the miraculous. The events of our week are his sketch pad. The steps of our obedience are his art pencils. The depth of our zest for life and living are the rich hues he colors. It is this passion for being alive that helps us find the mysteries of life. That inner fire unlocks the chains of drabness, lets us out of the prison of blandness, and puts a sunrise on the horizon. It was that passion that Edna St. Vincent Millay wrote of when she penned these lines:

> My candle burns at both ends;
> It will not last the night;

> But, ah, my foes, and, oh, my friends—
> It gives a lovely light.

A life filled with wonder gives a lovely light. It radiates. It glows. It gets back the sparkle of childhood.

Our psalmist was often astonished by God. Once he wrote in total awe, "When I consider your heavens, the work of your fingers, the moon and the stars, which you have set in my place, what is man that you are mindful of him, the son of man that you care for him?" (Ps. 8:3–4). Another time he said, "The heavens declare the glory of God; the skies proclaim the work of his hands. Day after day they pour forth speech; night after night they display knowledge. There is no speech or language where their voice is not heard" (Ps. 19:1–3). God's wonders increased the quality of his life.

It was Gilbert Chesterson who said, "The world will never starve for wonders; but only for want of wonder." Very true. It starves today, missing out not only on quality living but also on abundant living. Jesus came to give us overflowing fullness as 1 Corinthians 2:9 says: "No eye has seen, no ear has heard, no mind has conceived what God has prepared for those who love him."

How about that? God wants to surprise us. Sort of like little kids at Christmastime. Their eyes are wide, their expressions beyond words. It does something to the heart to see them opening up a new toy. Discovering a new gift. God wants life to have that kind of snapping-fresh crispness.

We need to stop aiming so low. Low is easy to hit. Aim higher! Give God a chance to astonish you. Don't pigeonhole him. Don't downplay the miracle power he has. Don't lose your awe of being alive.

> He takes the sound of the dropping nuts,
>   And the scent of the wine-sweet air,
> In the twilight time of the year's long day,
>   When the spent earth kneels in prayer,

113

He takes a thousand varied hues
  Aglow in opal haze,
The joy of the harvests gathered in—
  And makes the autumn days.

He takes the years—the old, the new,
  With their changing scenes and brief,
The close-shut bud and the fruiting bough,
  Flower and fading leaf;
Grace and glory and lack and loss,
  The song, the sigh, the strife,
The joy of hope and the hope fulfilled—
  And makes of the years a life.
                    —*Annie Johnson Flint*

Escape from fantasy island. Start wondering.

# 24 Praise

## Hallelujah Chorus

*Praise the LORD. Praise God in his sanctuary; praise him in his mighty heavens. Praise him for his acts of power; praise him for his surpassing greatness. Praise him with the sounding of the trumpet, praise him with the harp and lyre, praise him with tambourine and dancing, praise him with the strings and flute, praise him with the clash of cymbals, praise him with resounding cymbals. Let everything that has breath praise the LORD. Praise the LORD (Ps. 150).*

In this book's sidekick, *Proverbs for Graduates,* I introduced you to a fellow named John Ploughman. He doesn't really exist. "John Ploughman" was used by the famous Charles Spurgeon as a pen name in writing some satirical religious humor. In the

some barbs for people who have
rumblers:

ching: One dog will set a whole
course is to stay out of the way of a
the grumbles. . . . Goodbye, all ye
would sooner pick a bone in peace
ole.

this praise business a bit too far. It
lowout. One shouldn't froth at the
enerally speaking, turn into a zoo
r does deathly silent, almost mys-
Our Psalm promotes a balance—

ising God is not a favorite national
n cannot seriously praise God if he
ordes of people in a pickle. Even at
that, there are a good many Christians who are down in the mouth.
They don't have a positive word to say to, for, or about God. Further-
more, they think people who go around praising God are religious
cornballs—*undignified*. That's nothing new. The Bible records a few
such party-poopers.

Michal was like that. She was Saul's daughter and King David's
wife. The David of Goliath fame had since grown up and become a
holy terror, literally speaking. He was the army general and had
recaptured the sacred ark of the covenant (2 Sam. 6). David got so
happy bringing the ark home that he started praising God aloud.
Yeah, right out on Main Street. He was dancing around and singing.
Dancing? Well, more like leaping all over the place. I doubt if he was
"moonwalking," but he was definitely footloose.

Up in the window Michal watched with a smirk. The Bible says
"she despised him in her heart" (2 Sam. 6:16). Isn't that the pits?
Here was David trying to praise God, and his wife hated him for it.

That's bad news. She paid a dear price for her terrible hardness—no children. Michal was never allowed by God to have children. Principle: *People who are unwilling to give God the honor due his name later miss out on blessings to praise him for.*

Then there was Mrs. Job. Granted, her situation was tougher than rawhide leather. Her kids were dead. The farm was lost. Poverty had set in. Now, there sat her husband—a medical disaster. He had boils from head to toe and was scraping the ooze off with a piece of old broken pottery. Talk about gross! But listen to what he said: "The LORD gave and the LORD has taken away; may the name of the LORD be praised" (Job 1:21).

Mrs. Job wasn't nearly so optimistic. She gave him a pitiful look and said, "Are you still holding on to your integrity? Curse God and die!" (Job 2:9).

Job's answer is a classic. He said, "You are talking like a foolish woman. Shall we accept good from God, and not trouble?" (vs. 10). Principle: *Praise does not hinge upon how good things are going, but is directed toward the God who never changes.*

Let's not forget Jonah. He was the preacher who toured the digestive system of a whale before giving in to God's will. What was God's will? Preach to a wicked city called Nineveh. When he finally did, the whole metropolitan area repented—120,000 people converted! Did Jonah praise God? No. No? That's right—no! He went off and pouted because he thought they deserved to be destroyed. Great guy? Principle: *God is not like us, but is sinless, and he always does what is right. Instead of questioning him, we should be praising him.*

The group would not be complete without mentioning the Pharisees. The Pharisees were real losers, because they were fakes. They didn't want God to get the praise. If he got it, they didn't. In short, the Pharisees were glory hogs, so self-centered that praising God seemed quite absurd. Upon a number of occasions dazzling miracles happened right in front of their eyes. Did they praise God? No. They griped. "Hey, man!" they would yell at Jesus. "You shouldn't be doing that today. It's the Sabbath!" Never mind that a blind man was seeing his family for the first time. Never mind that a cripple had just finished running a four-minute mile. Never mind that a hopeless leukemia victim was donating blood to the local blood bank. The only parade the Pharisees were interested in was the one that gave them star billing.

Near the end of Jesus' earthly ministry, he came riding into town on a colt. The people were praising God like crazy. They were making a real racket, saying, "Blessed is the king who comes in the name of the Lord! Peace in heaven and glory in the highest!" (Luke 19:38). This did not set well with the Pharisees. They said, "Jesus, tell those friends of yours to shut up!"

The Lord's answer to those self-praisers gives me goose-chills every time I read it. He said, "I tell you, if they keep quiet, the stones will cry out" (Luke 19:40). Principle: *Even a heartless piece of cold rock knows better than to deny God the glory due his holy name.*

We can never praise God too much. There never comes a point where we can say, "Well, that's enough. There's my quota. Should hold me for about a week." If we could praise him every hour of every day, there would be an ocean full of praise untold. Because God is infinite, finite praise only scratches the surface.

> There is always something over,
>   When we tell of all His love;
> Unplumbed depths still lie beneath us,
>   Unscaled heights rise far above;
> Human lips can never utter
>   All His wondrous tenderness,
> We can only praise and wonder,
>   And His name forever bless.
>
> —*Margaret Barber*

Psalm 150 is a merry medicine for everyone with a bad case of the grumbles. Praising sure beats pouting. If you don't believe me, check with Jonah.

## Catch the Fever

*My heart grew hot within me, and as I meditate*
*burned; then I spoke with my tongue (Ps. 39:3).*

Once upon a time there was an old man v
to dig graves. Since he was not experienced at it, his
came out right. They ended up either too long, too dee
Late one afternoon he dug a grave too deep. After su
tired that he sat down in the hole to rest. Well, the old
to sleep. About half an hour later another man v
through the dark cemetery. By surprise, he fell into th
man had dug. Talk about frantic! This guy was jumpin
to climb out, but the hole was just too deep. Finally, h
in the cold, moist grave.

help!" he started yelling.

in a dark corner of the

immediately the other

t!

thusiasm. He got a heavy

her energy that only God

he wonder-filled world of

it must be fed to keep

friend of mine. He is one

I know. I mean, this guy is

is dreams. He's with God,

. He believes in a little

hip with Jesus Christ.)

ur job.)

goals to get anywhere in life.)

must be willing to be risky.)

eness (You must keep plugging away.)

you there. But, may I add, you need *enthusiasm's* help
ift the gears. Enthusiasm is a good kind of reckless
wildness. Not sinfulness. But risky. Enthusiasm gives
geous energy to shift into a higher gear. To attempt
alone fear is too big to try. Enthusiasm will not bow
ar of failure. It realizes, as someone has said, that "if
orses, beggers would ride." Nothing happens with
You've got to shift gears to get moving.
is positive. It feeds off the positive. It withers under
very time you cry a what's-the-use line, the spark in
ns. Think about yourself. The times when you were
times when your enthusiasm also went flat.

What is enthusiasm? Get this. It is derived from two Greek words, *en* and *theos*. Literally, they mean "in God." Paul said, "If anyone is in Christ, he is a new creation; the old has gone, the new has come!" (2 Cor. 5:17). Being "in Christ" wipes out the old, sinful, negative past and brings a fresh, enthusiastic beginning.

But remember, enthusiasm feeds on the positive. Give it a regular diet:

***Positive thoughts.*** "Whatever is true, whatever is noble, whatever is right, whatever is pure, whatever is lovely, whatever is admirable—if anything is excellent or praiseworthy—think about such things" (Phil. 4:8). Positive thoughts generate energy, and energy breeds enthusiasm. Pessimists are slow producers. Average optimists almost always outdo above-average pessimists. Grab this: the psalmist got his positive thoughts by meditating on Scripture.

***Positive tasks.*** Love what you do, and do it very well. Become the best at it. Ecclesiastes 9:10 says, "Whatever your hand finds to do, do it with all your might. . . ." Look for the silver lining in your job, search for the golden rainbow in your tedious classwork, dig for the buried treasure beneath your churning brains and guts—because if you don't look and search and dig, you're a goner. Your energy will run dry, because there are gobs of things to strip your gears. When energy goes, so does enthusiasm. When enthusiasm goes, you just blend in with the rest of the bland scenery.

***Positive tension.*** Spirited people know how to make pressure work for them. Instead of being cooked by pressure, they make a pressure cooker of their own. Proverbs 24:10 holds a dynamic though simple truth: "If you falter in times of trouble, how small is your strength!" Tame tension like the lion master tames the lion. If tension is given a free hand at growling, it will eventually bite your head off! But those same troubles, when given to God, can melt into energy.

> For every hill I've had to climb,
>     For every stone that bruised my feet,

For all the blood and sweat and grime,
    For blinding storms and burning heat
My heart sings but a grateful song—
    These were the things that made me strong!

For all the heartaches and the tears,
    For all the anguish and the pain,
For gloomy days and fruitless years,
    And for the hopes that lived in vain,
I do give thanks for now I know
    These were the things that helped me grow!

'Tis not the softer things of life
    Which stimulate man's will to strive;
But bleak adversity and strife
    Do most to keep man's will alive.
O'er rose-strewn paths the weaklings creep,
    But brave hearts dare to climb the steep.

**Positive tongue.** Bad-mouthing creates a monster down inside you. A fat, ugly beast that ruins the pleasant person you are meant to be. Jesus taught that "out of the overflow of the heart the mouth speaks" (Matt. 12:34). Cruel tongues flame from a heart of evil. No godly enthusiasm lives where Christ is treated as a stranger. Down in that kind of heart, the best one can become is a con artist. "In Christ" enthusiasm cares about people. It shows in the peppy words of encouragement that leap from the mouth.

Guard well thy tongue—
    It stretches far;
For what you say
    Tells what you are.

Catch the fever. You've been reading the ingredients. Glory, wonder, and praise—they all live in enthusiasm's neighborhood. They all promote a white-hot zest for life. A contagious, incurable fever that

122

drives its victims to mine the secret lode of riches for which the world hungers.

Shift your gears. Hurry, don't be late! Or the gravedigger will have a hole ready for you.

# 26 Creativity
## Color My World

*My heart is stirred by a noble theme as I recite verses for the king; my tongue is the pen of a skillful writer (Ps. 45:1).*

The tale is told of an old man and a young boy who were floating down a river together in a canoe. As they moved along, the old man reached out and snatched a leaf from the water. He held his eyepiece to his eye and looked at the leaf's size, shape, and color. Then he asked the boy, "Son, what can you tell me about these trees?"

The lad replied, "Nothing, I'm afraid. I haven't studied about trees yet."

The wise old gent was bothered by that. "Well, then, you have missed out on 25 percent of life." He flipped the leaf back into the slow-moving currents.

After a while the water got shallow in places, and the wise old man stuck his hand into the cool stream and pulled up a hand-sized rock. He held it toward the boy and said, "Boy, what do you know about rocks, soils, and such?"

The kid shook his head. "I haven't studied that either."

A splash jumped up off to the right as the old man threw the rock overboard. "Young fellow, rocks and soil are the earth. That's 25 percent of life. Now you're missing out on 50 percent."

The boy was quiet, dejected. Birds sang as the water gurgled them along. The sun began to sink and twilight crept in. Soon the stars popped out and the old man asked yet another question, "Son, what do you know about the stars and the sky, the planets and the moon?"

Again the boy was blank. An empty stare was fixed on his face when he replied, "Mister, I haven't studied anything about the heavens either."

The old man spoke sharply, "Boy, you don't know much of anything. The sky is another 25 percent. When it comes to 75 percent of life, you don't know so much as a single thing!"

All of a sudden they could hear a thunderous noise up ahead. The sound of water crashing and groaning low. The kid hollered, "Waterfall! Jump for your life and swim!"

"I don't know how to swim," the old man yelled back. "I've never studied that."

The boy answered quickly, "Mister, if you can't swim, you will lose 100 percent of life!"

There's a moral to that story. What can be learned from studying isn't always what makes life tick. The old man knew 75 percent of life, generally speaking. But the 25 percent he didn't know cost him his future. What is in the other 25 percent? Intangibles. Those are the little things. They can't be seen. They can't be touched. And they can be taught only in a limited way.

So what am I getting to? This. Creativity is an intangible. Creativity is to life what swimming was to that old man. It makes the whole difference in your future. If you never do anything with the other 75 percent of learning—if you never create with it or put it to work for you—life will slip into a deep whirlpool called BLANK. Like a plain white sheet of paper. Nice, and crisp, and smooth, and blank. It means nothing. It has nothing to show. It waits to be drawn upon, written upon, painted upon, sketched upon, colored upon.

Your life is like that. It waits to be colored. In case it hasn't dawned upon you, graduation is a megastep. You should have gotten some handy tools in school. Some of you will get more tools in colleges and technical or vocational schools. Great! But tools are for creating, and the creating is up to you. Only you have the power to make something of yourself. Nobody will or can do it for you. So, you're at sort of a turning point.

There's a terrific truth in 1 Peter 1:13! It says, "Prepare your minds for action. . . ." That's what makes the cream rise to the top. Creators always end up a cut above the average. Creativity is what gives the world its Thomas Edisons, Abraham Lincolns, Henry Fords, Eleanor Roosevelts, Elizabeth Barrett Brownings, Emily Dickinsons, Teddy Roosevelts, Mark Twains, George Gershwins, Douglas MacArthurs, Madame Curies, Benjamin Franklins, and Amelia Earharts. Those people were born to create. But guess what? Everybody is—including you!

You have your "thing." Maybe you're a good speaker. Or a poet. Or a singer. Or a musician. Or a writer. Or a composer. Maybe you're a thinker—then philosophize, or be a businessman, a lawyer, teacher, scientist, or computer wizard. Maybe you have gifted hands—then draw blueprints, paint portraits, build, be a skilled worker, or a doctor. But whatever you become, create!

Look around. God carved a beautiful world. He *created* it. Bulletin: he made us like himself. Within all of us lies this special ability to do something with nothing. To start from zero and forge ahead. Anybody who is willing to work at it can.

Here's a list of eight things that will make you creative. They all begin with "I." But don't be confused; we owe everything to God. Especially a sound mind. This is for everybody who thinks, "Well, I'm just not a creative person."

**Individuality.** Creative people milk other minds, but they learn to be themselves. It's easy to mope around, thinking you're a nobody. It takes courage to accept yourself—strengths, limitations, and all—and then truck on with confidence. Being yourself means being free to be daring, to try new untried paths, and even to fail. Because failing is a fast ticket to creating a way to win!

**Inspiration.** Can you let go of your emotions? Can you be moved? Can you be touched down inside? Or can you listen to a stirring song and stay unaffected? Or read a heartwarming story and remain cold? Or watch an inspirational program and go away insensitive? To create, you must be "inspirable."

**Imagination.** You have permission to daydream. To visualize your project. See mental pictures of what you'd like to do and of yourself doing it. However, don't let your imagination run away with itself. It might get lost.

**Intuition.** Listen to your instincts, your gut feelings. Intuition is cousin to imagination. It funnels insight into your dreams.

**Intake.** Before you can exhale, you've got to inhale. Absorb data. Keep educating yourself. Information breeds fresh creativity. Sponge up lots of stuff, and let it be fun.

**Ideas.** Don't be afraid to let your brain storm. Ideas come from inspired individuals who imagine—who listen to their inner feelings—who gorge themselves on info. Ideas swim in schools of dozens for creative people. To them every idea has possibilities.

**Inquiry.** "Why?" is a friend to hang on to. He teaches you to

127

investigate. To dig. To uncover. So ask questions. Pursue your dreams by exploring. Explorers almost always find something eventually, if they don't quit too soon.

**Invent.** Up to this point creativity has been swirling on the inside, aching to get out. When you capture the other seven, you will naturally do this last one. You'll produce. No problem. I know, because God created us to be creative. And I know, because I've had it happen to me. Once upon a time this book was nothing more than an inspired idea in my imagination. Individualism, intuition, and inquiry caused it to land on the page—an invention! Believe me, if I can do it, anybody can.

Jesus illustrated creativity in a parable. A certain master gave three of his servants some money according to their various abilities. One guy got around $5,000, another got $2,000, and the last got $1,000. (Read Matthew 25:14–30.) Then the master left, expecting his "stockbrokers" to be creative with the money.

When he returned, the first guy had smartly doubled his. How's that for profits? His name was E. F. Hutton. (No, not really.) The second guy doubled his, and got just as much recognition as the first. You see, the master was not as concerned with how much was returned as he was with what his servants did with what they were given. He had no respect for laziness or quitters.

The last guy? He bombed. Believe this? He took his money and buried it in a hole. Sure, he wasn't given as much as the other guys, but he didn't do anything with what he did have. What happened? He lost what he had.

Jesus was driving home a deeper lesson than being stock-market experts. He was saying, "Look! God has given everyone abilities. Don't waste them. Explore the possibilities. Use what talents you have to bless others. It brings you a rewarding life."

It's your life. God gave you some pencils and paints. Create, or the pages will end up blank. That would be about the same as riding over a waterfall. And not knowing how to swim.

# 27 Conquest

## Eye of the Tiger

*For he has delivered me from all my troubles, and my eyes have looked in triumph on my foes (Ps. 54:7).*

**R**ocky Balboa. A symbol of victory. Most people can relate to him, even though he's only a fictional character. Rocky was a boxer. You probably know all about him. How, as a no-name, he was given a shot at Apollo Creed's championship belt. How he lost in a bloody brawl. How he got a rematch and won.

In *Rocky III,* he loses the belt. Then he sets out to win it back. By this time Apollo Creed has retired from boxing and becomes Rocky's trainer. When Rocky doesn't catch on to the rigorous training schedule, Apollo tells him that he's going to lose. That he isn't hungry to win and doesn't want it badly enough. To inspire Rocky, Apollo gives him a slogan: "Eye of the tiger."

129

Our psalmist had that eye of the tiger. See it? He said, "My eyes have looked in triumph on my foes." God doesn't want us to be defeated, whipped, or wiped out. He wants us to win!

Joshua was a winner. Talk about a guy who could lead an army. Joshua mopped up in the Promised Land and led the people to their new home. God has a Promised Land for each one of us in this life. You don't have to wait until you get to heaven to be a conqueror. The question is: Are you willing to put up a fight?

Who are the enemies? Before I tell you, let me warn you. They're tough. They are capable of stomping us. In fact, without help we're no match for them. Trying to take them on alone will result in a first-round knockout every time. All three are super-heavyweights.

**The World.** I don't mean people, but the system, the philosophy of the world—living for pleasure and money. It includes materialism—craving possessions. Worldliness is never "next to godliness." Worldliness forgets God altogether.

James and John knew. James told us that "anyone who chooses to be a friend of the world becomes an enemy of God" (James 4:4). John said, "Do not love the world or anything in the world. If anyone loves the world, the love of the Father is not in him" (1 John 2:15). Take it from these brothers who were nicknamed the "sons of thunder"— the world is an enemy that spits poison darts.

> The world holds nothing so dear
> That Christ cannot give us more:
> His love, His peace, His joy—
> Far more than heart could implore.
> Our lives lose much He has for us
> As we cling to our earthly ties:
> In Him are pleasures forevermore,
> Let go—for Christ satisfies!

The world's battle tactic is to get you to play along. To go with the flow. It tries to make you look stupid if you're "different." Exodus 23:2

is a right hook to be used in the ring by any up-and-coming Rocky: "Do not follow the crowd in doing wrong. Do not pervert justice by siding with the crowd. . . ." Crowd-pleasers get bloody noses and busted lips, because the world will beat us up spiritually—if we let it.

**The Flesh.** No, not your skin. It's that inner competitor called Selfishness. He's a ringmaster. He knows just how to lure you into a trap. He knows your desires and how to corrupt them. Yes, at times you can become your own worst enemy.

Peter gives a trainer's pep talk in our corner: "Dear friends, I urge you . . . to abstain from sinful desires, which war against your soul" (1 Pet. 2:11). Sinful desires. That's the flesh.

> Didst not Thou die that I might live
> No longer to myself, but Thee,
> Might body, soul, and spirit give
> to Him who gave Himself for me?
> —*Charles Wesley*

Strategy to win? It's a mental trick. Die in your mind. *Die?* That's right. Crucify those selfish, sinful desires. After you die, you are ready to live a resurrection life! Galatians 2:20 is an uppercut to the flesh: "I have been crucified with Christ and I no longer live, but Christ lives in me. The life I live in the body, I live by faith in the Son of God, who loved me and gave himself for me." The loser in you has got to die so that the winner in you can live. It's all in your mind. That's where a lot of battles are won and lost.

**The Devil.** This isn't some cartoon character with horns, red skin, a long tail, and a pitchfork. That dumb idea causes us to underestimate his power. But before we give this creep too much credit, let's clear up one thing. The devil is a born loser. Oh, sure, he's dragging people into hell, which is awful! He's punching out a lot of Christians, too. However, someday God is going to crush him like a bug. There won't even be a contest.

131

The devil fights like a bully. He picks on us because he can't even touch God. It's like trying to get even with somebody by hurting their kids. Warped, huh? Well, that's what you're up against in the devil. Hate, pure hate.

One verse warns us about the devil's battle plan toward people: "Be self-controlled and alert. Your enemy the devil prowls around like a roaring lion looking for someone to devour" (1 Pet. 5:8). So, it's the prowling lion versus the eye of the tiger.

Thank God, Jesus is in our corner! Martin Luther said it best in his famous hymn, "A Mighty Fortress Is Our God." In the first stanza he reminds us how mean Satan is:

> For still our ancient foe
> Doth seek to work us woe;
> His craft and power are great,
> And, armed with cruel hate,
> On earth is not his equal.

But then he brings the battle into focus at the end of stanza three:

> The prince of darkness grim—
> We tremble not for him.
> His rage we can endure,
> For, lo, his doom is sure;
> One little word shall fell him.

I get spine-tinglers when we sing that song in church. I want to cheer, because I know I'm on the winning side.

We step into the ring every day. Any one of these three enemies—the world, the flesh, the devil—would be tough, but we fight all three at the same time. Every day. Sound unfair? The key to the match is letting God fight the battles for you, through you. If you do, you conquer! If you don't, you get smacked on the head—your spiritual head. Too many smacks can put you down for the count.

I remember when "Wide World of Sports" came on TV with the

phrase, "The thrill of victory and the agony of defeat." Feel that thrill of victory!

> To feel the tempter's mighty power—
> without appeal,
> To know the pull that money has—
> and never kneel,
> To be entranced by honor's glare—
> and have no urge,
> To hear the voice of passing pomp—
> and not submerge,
> To be uplifted, lauded high—
> and sense no pride,
> To gain an orator's great fame—
> and never stride,
> To be exalted to the skies—
> yet self disdain,
> To be condemned and set aside—
> and not complain,
> —THIS IS VICTORY!
>> —R. E. Neighbour

To taste the thrill of victory like this, you'll have to have Jesus fighting for you. Then you can raise clenched fists high, just like Rocky did, and say, "Thanks be to God! He gives us the victory through our Lord Jesus Christ" (1 Cor. 15:57). He gives you the eye of the tiger.

# 28 Blessings

## *From Eternity to Here*

*Praise the LORD, O my soul, and forget not all his benefits
(Ps. 103:2).*

One of the most heartwarming stories I've ever read
comes from a book by Howard Hendricks entitled, *Say It with Love*. A
Christian couple to whom he was ministering had fallen on some
hard times in the tight economy. Having four kids in the family made
things even tougher. One night the family was having a devotional
time when Timmy, the youngest, said he needed a shirt. So they put a
"size-seven shirt for Timmy" on the prayer list.

Day by day Timmy reminded everyone in the family to be praying
for his shirt. Several weeks passed. Then one Saturday a man who
ran a clothing store called the mother. He told her that he had just

finished his clearance sale and had some shirts left over that she could have for her boys. She asked what size. The answer came back clear as a bell—*size seven!* When she asked how many, he told her she could have them all—twelve!

That night, when devotion time came, the family couldn't wait to surprise Timmy. Once again he reminded everybody about his shirt. He didn't know what a plan they had cooked up for him.

When his mother said, "We don't have to pray for the shirt, Timmy," he wanted to know how come. She told him the Lord had answered his prayer. He was excited, as any little boy would be.

Here was the surprise plan that went into action. Timmy's brother Tommy goes out and gets one shirt. He brings it right over and lays it down on the table in front of Timmy. Then Tommy goes back out and brings back another shirt. Timmy's eyes are wide with astonishment. Tommy goes out and back, and out and back, until all twelve shirts are stacked in front of Timmy. That special plan was meant to show Timmy that there is a God up in heaven interested enough in Timmy's needs to provide him with shirts. Down to the exact size!

May I share a very important truth with you? God is not stingy. He wants to bless his children. He is eager to do so. On top of that, he promises to provide our needs for us. Listen, you couldn't even get a union to write you a better contract!

Still, we worry. How quickly we forget all that God has done for us, and *is doing* for us right now. Jesus pulled the plug on worrywarts. He said that worrying is senseless. Let his words sink in: "So do not worry, saying, 'What shall we eat?' or 'What shall we drink?' or 'What shall we wear?' For the pagans run after all these things, and your heavenly Father knows that you need them" (Matt. 6:31–32). In other words, God will bless and take care of you. He will provide.

He provided for Elijah. In 1 Kings 17 you can read about some of the most spectacular blessings ever. God sent Elijah to live by a brook. Then ravens carried him bread and meat every morning and every night. By the way, it might interest you to know that ravens are scavengers, flesh-eating birds. So it is no small miracle that they didn't rip off the food for themselves. God's blessings!

After a while the brook dried up. So Elijah was sent by God to a town called Zarephath. He went to mooch off this poor widow and her little boy. With only enough food left for one last meal, the poor widow expected they would starve to death. What did Elijah do? He said, "Give the food to me. I'm hungry." Nice guy, huh? Except that Elijah was in touch with a miracle-making, blessing-sending God. What happened? The widow's flour jar and oil jug would not run dry. That's right. She would pour them both empty, make a meal, and go back to find enough to make another meal. Blessing? Absolutely! And yet, she had to trust God from one meal to the next.

One of the most popular promises of blessing in the Bible is in Philippians 4:19. It says, "And my God will meet all your needs according to his glorious riches in Christ Jesus." That means food, clothes, house, transportation, money, education, friends, health, and so on. God will meet our needs.

I think it's important to point something out. Our "needs" do not always match our "wants"! Sometimes we feel as if God has been tight with his blessings, but that is usually us being gluttonous. Not just for food! Ask yourself if your "need" is really a need. Like:

Do I really need $350 a month for spending money at college?

Do I really need a Mercedes 450 SL?

Do I really need a $1,378 diamond ring?

Do I really need a $580-a-month apartment?

Exaggerations? Not for some people. My point is, we all get down-right greedy sometimes. We want to eat our cake and have it too.

You know what, though? God's blessings often far exceed our needs, and he gives us more than we deserve. See what our psalmist said? "Forget not all his benefits." God gives good fringe benefits. Three cheers for God for the ways he takes care of us.

After the three cheers, I've got three "beware"s. When God opens heaven and lets the blessings fly in our direction, there are some things to beware of:

***Beware of big-headedness.*** We can be so dumb. Can you believe that people actually try to take credit for something that's God-given? I mean, they didn't have anything to do with it. God blessed by his grace, but they've gotten a bit mixed up. To hear them tell it, it was all their doing. And 1 Corinthians 4:7 punches a hole in balloon-heads: "For who makes you different from anyone else? What do you have that you did not receive? And if you did receive it, why do you boast as though you did not?" That's something to chew on.

***Beware of bargain-making.*** It goes like this: "Dear God, if you'll do this for me, then I'll do this for you." God is not into swap meets. He's not a running flea market. He sets the conditions; we don't. When we state terms, we lose out. Because we always sell ourselves short. But God does not. By just reading Romans 5, you would find he's ready to give us "much more." Psalm 84:11 says that "no good does he withhold from whose walk is blameless." That's the best bargain you'll ever get. Just watch how you walk.

***Beware of stinginess.*** Stashing instead of sharing brings shortage. If you hoard God's blessings, they evaporate. Share them and they escalate. Ecclesiastes 11:1 promises: "Cast your bread upon the waters, for after many days you will find it again." Oftentimes it comes back buttered! If you haven't already heard—you can't out-give God!

Just ask Timmy.

# 29 Thanksgiving

## *From Here to Eternity*

*Give thanks to the LORD, for he is good; his love endures forever (Ps. 107:1).*

**B**ing Crosby, known as "The Crooner," once sang a song that has stuck in my memory. I often find myself crooning the tune. The words go like this:

> When I'm worried, and I can't sleep,
> I count my blessings
> Instead of sheep;
> And I fall asleep
> Counting my blessings.

It works like a charm. We all have more blessings than we can count. Trouble is, we've gotten so used to what we have that we've come to expect it, rather than appreciate it. We take it for granted. Result? In creeps ingratitude.

Ingratitude is a villain. A scamp. A rogue. A knave. It takes and wants more. It uses and walks away, not even looking back. Ingratitude is thankless and impolite. Although it receives huge bounty, far above average, it acts as if that's the way it should be. It never pauses to whisper a word. Then, should it be slighted in any way, it howls like a coyote. William Shakespeare wrote this about ingratitude:

> Blow, blow, thou winter wind!
> Thou art not so unkind
>   As man's ingratitude;
> Thy tooth is not so keen,
> Because thou art not seen,
>   Although thy breath be rude.

Catch that? Ingratitude has halitosis—bad breath!

Jesus dealt with ingrates. The ten lepers. Have you read their story in Luke 17:11-19? Well, if you haven't, don't get lepers confused with leopards. Leopards have spots on their skin, creating exotic beauty. Lepers have spots on their skin, creating decomposed ugliness. A leper has a disease that causes his flesh to rot off in mushy, mucouslike slime. Pretty gross, huh? And sad.

In this true story, Jesus healed all ten lepers miraculously. When one of them realized what had happened, he started yelling and ran over to Jesus. He fell down limp at the Lord's feet and thanked him. Jesus' answer was a sermon in itself, "Were not all ten cleansed? Where are the other nine?" Who knows? They probably rushed off to the camel races. Obviously, they thought they deserved the miracle, or else they would have at least been nice enough to send a thank-you card. Not even so much as a "good work, Jesus" was said.

The Israelites were ingrates in the wilderness. Get this. They were starving-to-death hungry. So they started whining and griping. God

139

sent some of his homemade bread to them. It was called manna. At first this manna stuff was novel, like angel food cake. But as anything with ingrates, it lost its value. They griped about that, too. "We want quail! We want quail! We want quail!" they chanted. God said, "Okay. Have some quail. Have so much it will run out your noses." Then he sent a quail blizzard to shut them up. When the storm ended there were quail three feet deep all over the camp. (Read Numbers 11:4–32 for the whole story.) But guess what? After a month of eating quail, they couldn't bear the sight of that bird. Fickle—ingrates are fickle!

There are virtually hundreds of things to be thankful for. That our basic needs are met should flood us with gratitude. However, there are some other things to which I want to draw your attention. Not to minimize God's daily provisions in our lives, but just to say, "Hey! Here are some things that get overlooked. Don't forget to offer thanks for them."

*Jesus.* Unexpected? He's the most forgotten blessing. He died and rose again, just so that we could be forgiven and build a friendship with God. He *is* salvation! Besides that, every day he's right on the spot to help us.

> What the hand is to the lute,
> What the breath is to the flute,
> What the fragrance is to the smell,
> What the spring is to the well,
> What the flower is to the bee—
> That is Jesus Christ for me.

> What's the mother to the child,
> What's the guide to pathless wild,
> What is oil to troubled wave,
> What is ransom to the slave,
> What is water to the sea—
> That is Jesus Christ to me.

> —*C. H. Spurgeon*

***The little things.*** God is always doing little things for us. No, they don't sound with a trumpet like good health and food and shelter do. They just poke their heads through the windows of life. They peek in right when we need them. Like a timely song, or extra miles out of tires that should have worn out long ago. A dog's kiss, or a cat's purring. A child's laughter. Double hot-fudge sundaes and Snickers candy bars. A memorable vacation, or an especially nice day. A good book to escape into. A quiet evening with a crackling fire in the fireplace. A stroll along the beach at dusk. A touching moment that lets you cry silent tears of joy in a world full of sorrow. A gentle rain. A purple sunset. Oh! These are the things that fill life to the brim! Being thankful for them reminds us to notice them.

***Special people.*** How terrible that God-sent people touch our lives and never get a "Thanks." What a shame that people we love do not hear our gratitude for what they mean to us. These anonymous lines cry out the regret of waiting until it's too late to show gratitude toward that special person:

> Over the casket pitiful we stand
> And place a rose within the helpless hand,
> That yesterday mayhap we would not see—
> When it was meekly offered.
> On the heart
> That often ached for one approving word
> We lay forget-me-nots; we turn away
> And find the world is colder for the loss
> Of this so faulty and so loving one.
> Think of the moment, ye who reckon close
> With love—so much for every gentle thought
> The moment when love's richest gifts are naught,
> When a pale flower upon a pulseheart lain,
> Like vain regrets exhaled its sweets in vain.

When I completed *Proverbs for Graduates,* I called one of my high-school teachers to tell her. She had greatly influenced me

141

toward writing, but I had not talked to her since I graduated. At first she didn't remember me. I expected she wouldn't. We took a few minutes getting reacquainted, and then I began telling her about the book and how thankful I was for her encouragement years ago.

As I was talking, I heard her crying softly. When I stopped to ask her what was wrong, she said, "In all the years I have taught, you are the first student to ever come back and say, 'Thank you.' If only you knew how many times I've felt like giving up, you'd know how much your phone call means to me."

I don't know about you, but I don't want to be like the nine lepers who forgot. Besides, counting sheep is a boring way to go to sleep.

# 30 Melody

## *Symphony of Living*

*Shout for joy to the LORD, all the earth. Serve the LORD with gladness; come before him with joyful songs (Ps. 100:1–2).*

Robert Louis Stevenson faced countless heart-wrenching difficulties in his life, not the least of which was physical disability. However, near the end of his life he said, "To miss the joy is to miss everything!"

Joy is the symphony of living. It is God's music concert in our hearts. Thousands of people never know the joy of a thrilling life. They live for the end of the workaday week—"Thank God it's Friday." Work is tedious to them, yet all off days are empty. One day they start remembering and have to think all the way back to high school to

143

find good memories. Graduation is supposed to be a beginning, not a dead end!

A teacher once told a student about to finish school, "Before you are finished, the world will do one of three things with you. It will make your heart very hard, it will make it very soft, or else it will break it. No one escapes!" He forgot one thing. God is in on this, too. If you let him, God will put a sound-recording into your heart that the world can never erase. A symphony!

However, that teacher was not all wrong. The world *can* harden you. It can fill the cassette tapes that play in your mind with sadness, gloom, dreariness, and blackness. Then comes drain pain. That's where you feel your motivation for living being sucked down the drainpipe. Into the sewer of grimness. We try to hide the pain. But when we do, it crushes the spirit—that driving force within.

Happiness. Everybody wants a piece of that pie. Guess what, though? You're absolutely right! Not many get hold of it. It seems slippery, always wanting to fall through our fingers.

Can I pass something along? Happiness is only one instrument in the orchestra. The whole symphony is designed around something much bigger—joy! For joy is so much more than happiness. Happiness only lasts so long as everything falls into place, but joy lodges deeper. People who find the secret of joy can be glad on the inside, despite what's happening on the outside. It goes like this: when happiness plays out of tune, it gets covered up by the rest of the orchestra. The symphony still sounds bravo!

Now, the question is: What is the secret of joy? Can everyone experience it? Sure! And guess what else? Joy is not a secret. God has hung it out in plain daylight.

**Be a branch.** Jesus said, "I am the vine; you are the branches. . . . I have told you this so that my joy may be in you and that your joy may be complete" (John 15:5,11). Branches cannot live without the vine. Have you ever seen a branch that tried to live its own way? It becomes firewood.

Imagine this scene. The branch wakes up one morning and says,

"I've had it, vine. I'm moving out. I'm going to start my own tree. I've got my own ideas on how to get fulfillment. So don't try to interfere. See me? Here I go. I'm packing my leaves." Silly, isn't it? Of course it is. Branches don't have the power to make it alone.

Exactly! Neither do we. People who want a symphony cannot hope to get it by playing solo. Abide in Christ! When the sap from the True Vine flows through us, the music can't be out-noised.

*Relax.* People are so uptight. Trying extra hard to be joyful doesn't get it. I'm afraid most of us take ourselves much too seriously. We are so intense, gripping life white-knuckle tight. Squeezing the "juice" out of each day won't give you a single glass of satisfaction. Not in a hundred years. Not in a million.

What we need to do is drink in the moments. Bask in the minutes. Paul wrote about this to the Philippians. From prison! "I have learned to be content whatever the circumstances" (Phil. 4:11). No wonder he could tell them, "Rejoice in the Lord always. I will say it again: Rejoice!" (vs. 4). In other words, "Relax! You guys are too caught up in living to enjoy life. Rejoice for a change."

*Laugh.* Sure, you heard me right. Fill up your place with big belly laughs. Just throw your head back and have yourself a knee-slapper. Good, clean humor is a medicine. Really? Read Proverbs 17:22: "A cheerful heart is good medicine."

God has a great sense of humor. Take a gander at creation. Have you ever looked a pig over real carefully? Funny, man. Very funny. The monkey. Now there's a born comedian if I ever saw one. Someone has said, "God has to have a sense of humor. He made us, didn't he?"

Go ahead and laugh. Especially, don't be afraid to laugh at yourself. It's a perfect way to turn goofs into gladness.

*Don't give in to gloominess.* A popular song once said, "Blues, blues, twentieth-century blues; nothing to win and nothing to lose." The blues are so bad. That's what Monday mornings are notorious for. The truth is that some people like being miserable. That's their way of getting attention. Dark old self-pity. The bluer the better. Isn't that sad?

Don't get me wrong. Somedays we feel flat. Out of gas. No-umph replaces triumph. Pretending as though everything is fine-and-dandy is just unrealistic sometimes. This is where the words of Habakkuk sound out with melody. Haba who? Habakkuk—one of the prophets hidden at the end of the Old Testament. Here's what he said. It's fantastic!

> Though the fig tree does not bud and there are no grapes on the vines, though the olive crop fails and the fields produce no food, though there are no sheep in the pen and no cattle in the stalls, yet I will rejoice in the LORD, I will be joyful in God my Savior. The Sovereign LORD is my strength; he makes my feet like the feet of a deer, he enables me to go on the heights. . . .
>
> Hab. 3:17–19

Wouldn't it be cool to glide through life with the graceful feet of a deer? Leaping tall buildings in a single bound? Breathing the freshness of life deep into your lungs?

Nehemiah 8:10 says that "the joy of the Lord is your strength." That principle should be tacked up on the refrigerator, or someplace we would see it every day. Because, as the symphony of joy ebbs low in us, we grow weaker and weaker. The devil likes that. He doesn't want anyone to have joy. You've heard of the Grim Reaper? Well, the devil is also the Grim Keeper. He will keep you grim—and weak—if you let him.

*Singing.* That's what comes out when the inside is full of joy. The music is spontaneous; it flows. Even though you can't carry a tune, you find yourself privately humming a melody. A joyful melody. The symphony is harmonizing on the inside.

Robert Ingersoll was an atheist. When he died, the funeral notices

146

read: "There will be no singing." How about that! Makes sense. I mean, what would they have to sing about? It is sad, though, that a man could live his entire life and never know the deep joy of living that God gives. To miss that joy is to miss everything!

# 31 | Life

## Not Just Another Cliché

*Show me, O LORD, my life's end and the number of my days; let me know how fleeting is my life. You have made my days a mere handbreadth; the span of my years is as nothing before you. Each man's life is but a breath. Selah (Ps. 39:4–5).*

Crowfoot was a warrior and orator for the Blackfoot Indians. When he died in 1890, these were his last words; "What is life? It is the flash of a firefly in the night. It is the breath of a buffalo in the wintertime. It is the little shadow which runs across the grass and loses itself in the sunset."

What can I say about life that hasn't already been said? In my research I came across over a thousand famous quotes about life. And you know what? Less than half were original. The other half were repeats of the first half.

Here you are graduating and, to be sure, that is the threshold of life. But everybody's telling you that. "Today is the first day of the rest of your life" and other clichés fill graduation cards, speeches, and promos from college recruiters. Life . . . ughhh! Getting tired of hearing about it? I don't blame you.

Can I pull you aside for a second, though? Life is not just another cliché. It's much, much more than any quote, poem, or song could describe. In fact, I've had my doubts about writing a chapter on it. A short chapter like this could never paint the broad canvas called life.

On the other hand, this is sort of a summary chapter, since we've been talking all about life as we journeyed along. Remember? This has been an adventure. We began way back there in chapter one at that old house with crumbling foundations. And, oh, the sights we've seen!

We climbed up that huge mountain of confusion—life is so confusing sometimes—and came real close to some answers. We gazed across the miles of life and saw the ruling sovereignty of God. But that was not as hard as looking into the mirror—at self!

The day we walked across that desert was pretty tough. Talk about thirstiness! But it was worth it, because we came to the land of ahhhs! It was quiet there and cool. And we learned to meditate by the whispering brook called Selah. We were overshadowed there. Remember? Glance back to chapter eleven. You'll see. We've kept a journal of our travels.

That rickety bridge. Remember it? We stopped as we came across and looked down. The rushing water reminded us that when God forgives us, it's like that cleansing water under the bridge. The flowers of hope were in full blossom on the other side. Just then we stepped into the twilight zone! Wasn't that scary?

It was at about this point that we threw up our hands in futility. Were we going in circles? Life does feel as if you're going around in circles sometimes. Finally, we began charting out our destiny.

How exciting! We took off like gangbusters. But our urgency got us in too big of a hurry. It was nice to slow down and unwind, to feel serene. Except! Loneliness trailed us for a while. And then we met that guy with all the casts on his arms and legs—brokenness. Remember him? Wow!

We'd have never made it if we hadn't stopped to learn about prayer. That's when we skyrocketed over that rainbow—glory! The wonders we saw left us praising, when before we didn't even know what praising meant.

The next town we came to—Enthusiasm—was probably the "jumpingest" place you've ever been. When you caught the fever, it looked for a minute as if you were going to color your whole world in a flash of creativity. A painter's fire burned inside you, I guess, because for the first time I saw you start to dream. Never, please, never stop dreaming. When the dreaming stops, the dying starts. Life ends!

Maybe the most spine-tingling place we adventured into was the fighting arena. That tiger and that lion. How fierce the battle was! I couldn't believe the tiger won. He was so much weaker; he must have had help. But I'll never forget the look you got in your eyes when you looked into his eyes—the eye of the tiger!

The next couple of days we went to eternity and back again on the wings of two mighty eagles—Blessings and Thanksgiving. The whole adventure touched off a symphony down inside. A symphony of what living is all about.

Snap! Snap!

"Hey! Wake up!"

"What?"

"Wake up. You've been dreaming."

Yes, you've only gotten a tiny peek at the things life has to offer. We've been traveling and adventuring only in our imaginations. Not too long from now, though, your imagination will change into reality.

By now you've probably moved your tassel. Thrown confetti into the air. And celebrated. Now it's time to begin. Suddenly the journey ahead looks long, frightening. Just remember, you can sneak a look back through our little travel log. Any time you want to. It might give you a preview of things to come.

As the door of life swings open for you—and you take those first few steps into your future—let me leave you with a few thoughts. It's the least you could allow a fellow traveler like me:

*Love life.* Sound corny? I don't mean for it to. Psalm 34:12 says it's good to love life. Sure, sometimes life is a bear. Growling and impossible to contend with. But, still, nothing is so precious as life. I can't understand why some people want to blow themselves away. I don't know how to describe what loving life feels like. But it *is* a great feeling! It's the sort of feeling that makes your heart feel as if it's swelling up with joy.

*Handle with care.* Life is fragile. Carelessly lived, it smashes into smithereens. Proverbs 19:3 says, "A man's own folly ruins his life." Throwing life around like American Tourister luggage will send you packing your bags in the truest sense of the word. Broken pieces are hard to mend. But we saw that in the chapter on brokenness, didn't we?

*Lose your life.* What? Easy now. Let me explain. Jesus once said, "Whoever finds his life will lose it, and whoever loses his life for my sake will find it" (Matt. 10:39). Oh, yeah? What's that mean? This: when a person concentrates only on self—getting into what "I" want—his or her life disintegrates into nothing. But if you are absorbed in Jesus Christ—and lose all personal claim to your own life—you find out what living is all about. Lose your life in Jesus Christ. That's what is meant by: "For you died, and your life is now hidden with Christ in God" (Col. 3:3). Tough to grasp? I know it is. Maybe this is the best way to say it: "Abandon yourself. Forget yourself. Then Christ will give you the desire for a thrilling life that burns like a fire within. You'll find life!"

*Mist evaporates quickly.* We are asked: "What is your life? You are a mist that appears for a little while and then vanishes" (James 4:14). Here comes a cliché I can't resist, because it's so true—life is

151

short. If that's hard to understand, just ask an elderly person about it. Someone like old Crowfoot.

Or watch the little shadows run across the grass into the sunset. Step into an amazing world—and have an amazing life!